# THE
# OLD
# FELLOW'S
# WAR

# THE OLD FELLOW'S WAR

## A TRUE STORY

### BY EDMOND NYST

NEW
HOLLAND

First published in Australia in 2007 by
New Holland Publishers (Australia) Pty Ltd
Sydney * Auckland * London * Cape Town
1/66 Gibbes Street Chatswood NSW 2067 Australia
218 Lake Road Northcoate Auckland New Zealand
New Edgeware Road London W2 2EA United Kingdom
80 McKenzie Street Cape Town 8001 South Africa

Nyst, Edmond.
    The old fellow's war : a true story.

    Includes index.
    ISBN 9781741105827 (pbk.).

    1. Nyst, Edmond.  2. World War, 1939-1945 - Personal
    narratives, Dutch.  3. World War, 1939-1945 - Personal
    narratives, Australian.  4. World War, 1939-1945 -
    Underground movements - France.  5. World War, 1939-1945 -
    Europe - Personal narratives.  6. World War, 1939-1945 -
    Pacific Area - Personal narratives.  7. Soldiers -
    Australia - Biography.  I. Title.


    940.5481

Publisher: Martin Ford
Project Editor: Lliane Clarke
Design: Tania Gomes
Production: Linda Bottari
Printer: Griffin Press, Adelaide, South Australia

# CONTENTS

# PROLOGUE

All of a sudden I find myself writing about events that I have tried all my adult life to forget. It came about one afternoon when my son Malcom dropped in for a cup of coffee. He, my wife and I were talking about a book written by a ninety year old man about the First World War and his participation in the ANZAC landing at Gallipoli. 'You should do the same thing, Dad.' And my wife, an ex-archivist and librarian, emphasised that older people have a duty to the future generations, each in their small way, to contribute to the history of their period. 'Who the hell wants to hear about the old fellow's war?' was my reply.

'I for one,' said Malcom. 'When you die, it all goes with you.' So what? I wasn't convinced then, but I did think about it for a couple of days and one morning, not having anything more important to do I sat in front of my computer and began to wonder. Where does one really start? Logically, I suppose one should start at the beginning. So, for what it's worth, here goes!

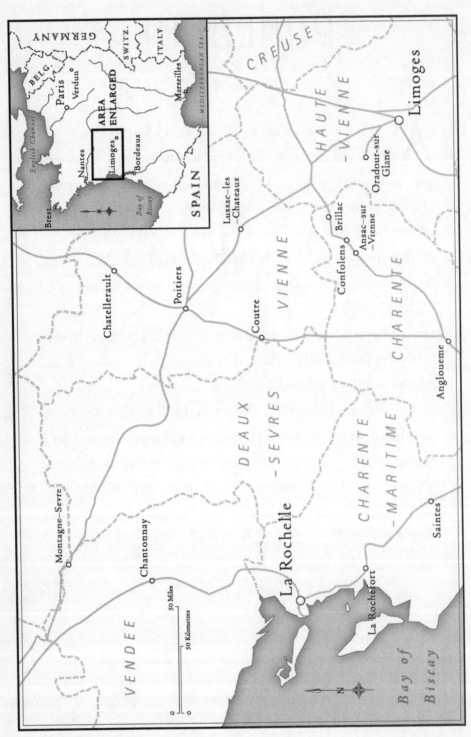

Central France

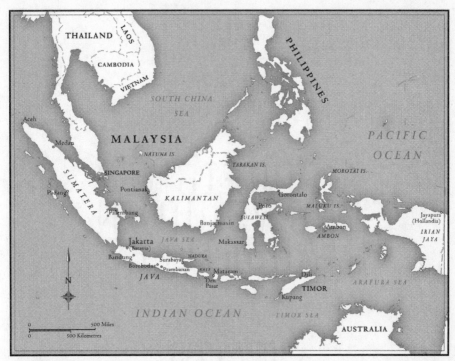

Malaysia

Timor

# 1

# A FOREIGNER GROWS UP IN MARSEILLES

## 1927–1939

I was never French. Although I was born in France, I did not, thankfully, ever come to truly qualify for the ethnic label that English speaking people like to refer to, as Frenchies or Froggies when they speak in derision about a national of that country. I must admit that never at any time at school, or at any other place where kids play, was I not made vividly aware that I was *un étranger*, a foreigner. One of those horrible creatures, according to some of the more vociferous young *patriôtes*, who sneaked into France to '*boufer nôtre pain*'; eat our bread.

It was 1934, I was seven years old. In those early days of the great world depression when poverty was rampant and many people went hungry; what the French kids heard their fathers say at home, they felt justified to express in public. Particularly at me since I was, in their view, one of 'those horrible creatures'. Of course that did nothing to spark in me, as a young child, nor later in life, the flame of patriotism which should have warmed my heart with love and admiration for my adopted country. I hated it and them. All except one, good old George, but more about him later.

Being ostracised by my contemporaries from such a tender age I reacted introspectively. I developed a reactionary attitude towards people and opinions, an attitude, which sometimes has served me well. But an attitude which, also, on many occasions, got me into a lot of trouble. Anyway I grew up to be independent, defiant, arrogant at times, encrusted in my own opinions, a real smart-alec so to speak, but that did not bother me. I had grown immune to derogatory remarks and frivolous comments. I was me. I must have been a real pain in the a…, as people often rightly accused me of being. But it was water off a duck's back. I did not care. I did not believe them. Anyway as I said before, I was me. I accepted myself as I was.

My father was the Dutch Consul in Marseilles. Also a foreigner. He had been there since before I was born. It was there that he met my mother. She also was a foreigner. *Une étrangère*. She was born in New York and came to France as a little girl when my grandfather decided to settle there at the end of the First World War. Neither he nor my grandmother, who was from Italian descent, ever surrendered their American nationality. They died American. So as you can see, we were all foreigners in France, the entire family.

From my father I learned justice, morals and integrity. From my mother I learned to cook lovely plates of pasta. At school I learned to swear and in the streets I learned to fight. I also learned something else in the street and that was from one of the big boys. He knew everything; so he should, he was twelve years old. We were all around him that day, all boys, five or six of us, all listening to him with our mouths wide open. He was telling us how babies are born. 'It's only the women', he was saying 'their belly is full of these small things, they look like leeches. They float around in there and then from time to time one of them grows into a baby and comes out.

'Where?'

'From their back side.' Of course those of us boys who did not have sisters did not know that the front side of girls was different from ours. Nevertheless I must admit that this explanation of how babies were born made a lot more sense to me then than the one that my mother had told me about the cabbage patch. But I never told her that. I never told my mother that now I knew all about it.

In those days the world was small and people didn't know much. We lived in a nice villa in a suburb of Marseilles called Mazargue. It was like a small village. There was a tram going from there to the city where the Dutch Consulate was and my father would commute with it every day except Sunday. He did not have a car. In fact I never saw my father drive. He had some kind of arrangement with a limousine company which would supply him with the same car and the same chauffeur whenever he had to attend any formal function. My brother and I hardly ever went to Marseilles; Mazargue was our domain. We both went to the local school where we didn't learn very much, but of course in those days there wasn't very much to learn. The teachers had no formal training and what they lacked in ability to teach was not compensated by any other qualities. Although my brother was a few years younger than I was, we were both in the same classroom. Come to think of it the school only had two classrooms and a very small play yard with standing room only for the kids.

On the way home from school I used to watch various tradesmen at work. Most workshops were fully open directly on to the street and one could stand there and watch them work. Two of them really fascinated me, the cooper and the blacksmith. My brother wasn't particularly interested. He would go on home on his own while I would spend hours in front of these workplaces picking my nose and watching them work. I learned a lot. I was amazed the way the cooper would line the shaped plank around what was going to be one of the lids, secure them with a metal ring and then light a big fire underneath to bend the planks inwards. Then he would turn the whole thing upside down and with a rope and more metal rings he would bend the other ends of the planks inwards and lock in the other lid. A few hits of the rings with a punch and a hammer and there it was, a beautiful new barrel ready for the wine.

I also learned a lot from the blacksmith. His workshop was beside an empty lot. There were always three or four large Clydesdale type horses waiting there, just like one waits at a barbershop for a hair cut. From time to time the blacksmith would come out of his workshop with a red hot horse shoe held between long black pincers and would try it for size on one of the horse's hooves. It was always too small. This operation made a little smoke and smelled funny. Watching this I would cringe, but the horse didn't seem to mind. They were brave animals these horses. It was all very interesting to watch. After that the blacksmith would dip the hot shoe into a bucket of cold water and then he would nail it straight under the horse's foot with long square nails. There again the horse did not seem to mind. When that was done, with a chisel and a hammer, he would trim the horse's foot to the size of the shoe. Watching this I was glad that they did not use the same method when my mother took me to buy a new pair of shoes.

Sometimes, the tinsmith would come around. He was a gypsy with long black hair like a horse's tail and a face that looked as if it had been shaped with an axe. He also spoke funny. He would go from house to house collecting ladles, forks, copper saucepans and other utensils to be re-tinned. Then he would light a wood fire in the gutter and get to work. Kids would come over and watch. The sight of this strange sorcerer bent over his magic cauldron full of liquid metal fascinated us; especially because he was telling us that the metal in the cauldron was pure silver. And we had no reason to doubt him. Waaho!

When I was nine, we moved to Marseilles. There we lived in a very large apartment very close to the centre of the city where the Dutch Consulate was. In order to get away at weekends, which meant from Saturday night till Monday morning, my parents also bought a small farm at a place called Allauch. It was about twelve miles from Marseilles and like Mazargue, Allauch was also serviced by a tram. The farm was called the Merlaou because the share-cropper who actually worked the farm was called Merle. Many generations of Merles had worked that farm for the previous four hundred years and it was only natural that their name had stuck to it. We, even though we owned the place, only used a small section of the behemoth farm building as a weekender. We had a separate entrance. The main room was the kitchen. It served also as lounge and dining room. In the kitchen corner of it was the fireplace where my mother cooked, either on grills straight over the wood fire or in saucepans hanging over the fire from a hook somewhere in the chimney. There were also two bedrooms but no electricity and obviously no gas. Bottled gas didn't exist in those days.

As I said before, in those days the weekends started at 7pm on Saturday evening. We were lucky; we could get away from the city. Come 7.30pm we were already in the tram bound for our little place at the farm in Allauch. Once there my mother would light innumerable numbers of candles, she missed electricity; while my father and we kids would try to get a wood fire going so my mother could cook dinner. We missed the gas. The entire exercise was challenging; it was *la campagne*, the country life. Although I must admit it at night it was very miserable. During the day of course it was quite different. We had plenty of space to play and run and do odd jobs on the farm. We thought it was great.

In the summer during the school holidays, Merle's grandchildren would come and stay at the farm and with some of the neighbours' kids we made quite a troupe. There were always about twelve of us, boys and girls. It was also during one of these summer holidays that my brother and I discovered that although the girl's backside was the same as ours, their front side was quite different. Like my little brother told my mother that night, 'there's nothing there, how do they pee?' That is also when my mother finally had to come clean as to how you can tell a girl from a boy when they are tiny little babies, when they all look the same.

She had previously told us that when they're first born the doctor looks inside their nose and he can tell whether the baby is going to grow into a boy or a girl. I was glad that this mystery was finally resolved. Being the little Know All that I was, I was getting quite a complex about not being able to spot that difference in babies' noses up to then. And boy had I looked! By the way, by then we had a new baby in the family and boy was I pleased that now I knew that it was going to grow into a second brother.

The move to Marseilles also necessitated a change of school. Education was becoming important and I was sent to a Catholic private school. It was the sort of institution where the hooligans came from good families. It was run by the Jesuits, God bless them! That I didn't mind so much, what I did mind was the manner by which they were trying to make me see the Light. Being educated by the Jesuits of course included in the curriculum long depressing sessions of Catechism. This had to do with the omnipotent power and ubiquitous presence of the All Mighty.

Of course, young me, the smarty, I did have a lot of intolerable questions to ask. Questions, which I later learned to my detriment, should not, under any circumstances, ever be asked, especially not during Catechism. They were questions, which had to do with common sense, and in the Catechism period one did not ask questions which had to do with common sense. That was it. The Father, judging by the type of questions I was asking, very soon discovered that my religious faith was abominably lacking. I found myself in deep trouble. You see, at that age I didn't know that when it comes to religion, questions which have to do with common sense should never be asked, they're taboo. I didn't know that common sense has nothing to do with religion and vice versa. So in order to guide me in the right direction I was made to kneel on my knuckles in the passageway until I would distinctly see the Light. Of course I never did see the Light but that exercise taught me to lie. I learned to pretend.

It was at that school that I met George. George Pannetier and I shared the one desk. They were desks made for two and the classroom was full of them. George also was a bit of a rebel and that is why our desk was right in front of the teacher's. 'So that I can keep an eye on you' was the warning he gave us. George and I became very good friends. We shared a lot of views in the different things that beset eight years old kids and very rarely did they coincide with what was expected by the establishment. We got into a lot of trouble because of it, but since he and I usually shared the two top marks our individual reputations were not too badly damaged. Some of the other kids did eventually look up to us. The school hours were long and monotonous. From eight thirty in the morning until seven at night, with two hours for lunch. The week ended Saturday night at 7pm but we did have Thursday afternoons off.

George's father was the general manager of the Marseilles Opera House and George and I often had the complimentary use of his father's private box at the Opera for the Thursday afternoon matinée. Even as kids we loved operas. But it wasn't always opera, sometimes it would be the rendition of some of the great French classics, works by Moliere, Corneille or Racine. They were the French equivalent of Shakespeare's plays. During the intervals some of the spectators would turn around and look at us rightly wondering what these two kids were doing in the presidential reserved box. We of course would play the part, as we had been instructed to do by George's father. Although we would be carrying on as normal kids during the performance, during the intervals when people were looking at us we would try to impress them by looking as dignified and majestic as we possibly could. We would always bring afternoon tea with us and during the boring parts we would sit on the floor where we could not be seen and share our delicacies. We knew most of the operas by heart and knew by the music when it was time to get up, sit on the chair and watch the gruesome bits.

There were by then quite a number of cinemas in Marseilles but we were not allowed to go unless one of our parents had seen the movie and judged it suitable. Even then we weren't allowed to go by ourselves, we had to be accompanied by one of our parents or grandparents. In 1937 my grandmother took us to see Errol Flynn in *Robin Hood*, and that was in colour. *Snow White* didn't make the cinemas for quite a few years later. We lived well, we were happy and we had plenty to eat. All that was soon to change.

# 2

# FRANCE GIVES IN
# TO THE NAZIS

## 1939–1940

It was also during one of these long summer holidays at the farm that our lives suddenly changed. It was in 1939. At the beginning of September. It was a Sunday. My father had gone to the village to get some groceries and came back with a special edition of the newspaper. The war had started. Hitler had marched his troops into Poland and England had declared war on Germany. France had also declared war on Germany a few hours later.

On that nice hot summer day, as we sat down to a nice al fresco Sunday lunch on the veranda, we were at war. My father was very concerned but my brother and I were thrilled to bits. We had heard my grandfather, the American one, talk about what he did during the Great War and we were excited by the idea that all this was coming back all over again.

That afternoon, my father had a long talk with Merle, the share-cropper. He was a veteran of the First World War and had three sons. One, Gabby, worked on the farm with him. The other two, Ernest and Louis, worked for the tramway company. That afternoon, we the boys of the troupe, sat together and talked about what our grandfathers had been through in the trenches of Northern France during the Great War. That evening was very sad. My mother was very upset. She kept bringing up the subject of toxic gases used during the last war. And also the fact that Marseilles being such a big city and the most important port on the Mediterranean was bound to attract severe bombing by the Germans. Would they use gas bombs?

One night, a week or so later, while we were having dinner the air-raid alarm sounded in Allauch. My mother was of course by then well prepared to cope with it. During the previous weeks she had purchased several tons of rolls of sticky tape and even before the sound of the siren stopped all of us were actively sticking tapes on top of every door and window joints to keep out the toxic gases. We had been at it for well over an hour and had not quite completed the job when the end of the alarm sounded and we had to unstick it all again. As we learned the next day it had been an exercise to test people's response.

We were due to go back to school on 1 October. In order to spare us kids the horrors of war in the big city my father decided to send us to the village school instead of back to the Jesuits. My brother and I originally thought that it was indeed a very, very, very good idea. As it turned out later it was a fiasco.

The kids at school could all speak French but amongst themselves they only spoke Provençal, the local dialect. We did not understand them. In the classroom the teacher used to insist that they spoke French.

'Tell your parents to speak French all the time at home,' he would say, but some of the kids would tell him 'But sir, my mother doesn't speak French, she only speaks Provençal.' We stayed at that school for a couple of months, we learned nothing there except to speak a little Provençal. In the end my father decided that war or no war it was better for us to resume our education in a proper environment and thus we were back at the Jesuits. Dam'hem!

The war had not really had any significant effect on our existence. There had been no other air alarms, tests or otherwise. Shops were full of whatever they were selling. There were no lists of casualties in the newspapers, in fact it was almost as if the war had died a natural death. People hardly spoke about it anymore.

I had bought a large map of France adjoining Germany and with it came a collection of little paper French, English and German flags stuck on a pin. I had hung that map at the back of my bedroom door. The little flags were pinned on the various positions held by the Allies or the Germans. These damn little flags didn't seem to move much. I remember a place that I had never heard of before called Sarrebruck, I had no idea whether it was originally French or German but all I knew was that its little flag was changing nationality every three or four days. All the other flags didn't seem to move at all. In the end I lost interest and forgot about the map and the little flags.

Soon after going back to school in Marseilles we were issued with gas masks. To make sure that they fitted properly the issuing party would stick one over our face and plug off the air intake with his hand. If you turned blue and your eyes disappeared from their sockets it was a proper fit. We hated the damn things. They came in a round tin with a sling to fit over your shoulder. Sometimes we had drills and with them on we had to walk down stairs to the cellars. They were now called shelters, as in air raid shelters. The transformation was purely semantic since no evidence of structural reinforcing had ever taken place.

And so the war went on. Merle's three sons had been mobilised. Two of them had been sent North, one as a stretcher-bearer to the front, the other I don't know what as. The third was stationed at an anti-aircraft battery somewhere along the coast not far from Marseilles. Christmas 1939 came and went. It had been an ordinary Christmas, not really affected by the war. People were trying to estimate how long it was going to last. All had different views but all agreed that it would be over within three months. Once Hitler secured the Danzig corridor from the Poles they were sure the war would end. We could not stop him from taking the corridor from this end of Europe and who the hell really gave a damn about the Danzig corridor anyway?

So slowly came Spring with its fine sunny days and warmer weather. The south of France was again at its best. Then one day, in May 1940, in the middle of that beautiful spring the war changed. German troops and tanks, circumventing the Maginot Line which had held them at bay until then suddenly invaded Holland and Belgium. The Blitzkrieg had started. Within a couple of weeks Holland and Belgium had been taken. The British Expeditionary Forces had been pushed back and isolated near Dunkirk. Paris had fallen. In the newspaper there was a photo of Hitler standing in front of the Arc de Triumphe in Paris and along the Atlantic coast the Germans had reached the Spanish border. By then I had long run out of little German flags to stick on the map behind my door. Those who had estimated that the war would be over within three months had been right. But not for the same reasons.

On 10 June the Italians crossed the border at Vintimiglia and invaded Provence. The French government in desperation immediately recalled an ex-First World War hero, Marshall Petain, and made him President of France, or what was by then left of it. He, in turn, appointed Pierre Laval as Prime Minister of the French Republique. They were both German sympathisers. This 'pair' turning their back on France's former allies immediately negotiated an independent armistice with the Germans. The terms of this armistice included full cooperation by France to the German war effort. In return Germany would leave a small portion of France unoccupied, to be ruled by these two scoundrels not from Paris but from a new capital called Vichy.

To my father's and my entire family's disgust most of the French people at the time applauded the dealings of this old traitor. One of them however resisted. His name was De Gaulle; an unknown French general who had slipped away to England at Dunkirk. On 18 June, De Gaulle from England, called upon the people of France not to surrender, telling them that the war was not over and that the Allies would eventually win. His call was ridiculed by the majority of the French people who still had great faith in Petain. And so it came to pass that the French population was now ideologically divided, unfortunately far, much too far from being equally divided. Most of them trusted Petain blindly and saw France's alliance with Germany as the only means of saving a little national pride. But there were a few, only a few, who, still feeling committed to France's allies, surrendered their faith to De Gaulle. Unfortunately at that time they were only a miserable few. We, my family, although none of us French, shared the feelings of these miserable few. We were with them.

It did not take long to discover that this 'Honourable Armistice', as it was now called by the majority of French people, was a joke. The entire French Government, in order to ingratiate themselves with the conquerors, became German puppets. Their zeal at times exceeded that of the Nazis. Particularly when it came to the Jews. France was a Catholic country and even before the war started a large number of French people quite openly declared that they shared Hitler's view on anti-Semitism. A statement which also was often heard in shops and in cafés was 'After all, it is the English who have been our enemies throughout history, not the Germans.' The French police also appeared to have adopted this misconceived loyalty, in any case either by duty or by faith, they openly behaved in a way which indicated that they were quite prepared to enforce the Vichy Government's view on the 'Jewish problem'.

Starting on 16 July 1942, the Paris police and *gendarmes*, in order to gratify the German authorities, went around the city and in two days arrested 3031 Jewish men, 5802 Jewish women and 4051 Jewish children. They were all taken to the cycling stadium at Drancy on the north side of Paris and later deported to the extermination camp of Auschwitz. This was done by the very same policemen and gendarmes who later, to save their faces in 1945, when the Americans were at the gates of Paris and the Boches were running for their lives, supposedly heroically freed the city from the German invaders. What a revolting mockery. They should all have been arrested and shot. What a short memory the French people had. Or was it perhaps that most of them still remembered when they had felt that Petain had done the right thing to turn his back on his Allies and help Germany win the war. In the light of how they once felt about it they were obviously quite prepared to forgive and forget.

By now, in the eyes of the new French Government, Holland and Belgium had ceased to exist. They were now part of Germany. The French authorities decided that a Dutch Consulate no longer had any *raison d'être*. My father still retained the premises but the Dutch Consulate sign and the Dutch flag had to be taken down. Instead my father decided to call the premises 'Bureau for Dutch Refugees'. And there were a lot of them. Many had escaped from Holland in front of the German army and had eventually drifted to Marseilles in the hope of catching a boat to the United States. Most of them were Jewish; ex diamond dealers or cutters from Amsterdam. Others were professors or lecturers from Leiden or other famous Dutch universities.

There were even, amongst them, a few Dutch Catholic priests and some ordinary people who for one reason or another had chosen to leave their homeland rather than to live under the Nazi's regime. Of course all of these people were to be disappointed very quickly. For a start there were no longer any boats leaving Marseilles for the United States. Next they discovered that the French authorities' attitude towards the Jews was equal if not worse than that of the Germans in Germany.

Many pathetic stories came to my father. Entire families were being arrested by French police and immediately deported to Germany. Of course in those days most people didn't know about the concentration camps. My father and I knew. One Sunday afternoon we went to visit a Dutchman who had been arrested in Marseilles and placed in a concentration camp at a place called Les Milles, very close to Aix en Provence. Before the war it had been a tile factory; now it was fenced with barbed wire and contained many hundreds of people. I didn't go inside, only my father did. Apparently one poor devil had been arrested by the French police on suspicion of being a Jew.

He had requested a contact with a Dutch official and the police had chosen my father. Apparently two policemen in civilian clothes had approached him in the street, had led him into a doorway and had asked him to show his penis. Because he was circumcised he was arrested. This practice was quite current in Marseilles and all other large cities. As it turned out, this man easily convinced my father that he was not a Jew, but before my father could do something about it the poor devil was deported to Germany and was never heard of again. So we knew about concentration camps but of course we knew absolutely nothing about gas chambers and the systematic extermination of detainees. How could a normal human being ever suspect such a thing. Even when the proof finally came out it was hard to believe.

This unfortunate episode at Les Milles concentration camp was only one of many events which came to my father's attention during those days. Some were even of people that we knew or had known socially, kids we had played with. They and their parents had suddenly disappeared never to be heard of again. Some of them we had not even known that they had been Jewish. We used to talk about it a lot at home. We could not understand why the French authorities were so keen to impress the Nazis. One day my father decided to do something about it. Having been all over the place before the war looking at farms before he decided on the one in Allauch, my father had a good recollection of some old, out of the way derelict farm houses which would serve his purpose.

Having first established that the owners of these dilapidated old places were either some of the 'miserable few' or those whose loyalty to the Vichy cause was at a price that my father could afford, he rented as many of these old places as he could find. There he installed the Dutch and other Jewish refugees who came to his attention. Because he knew the region so well he had them stabled in small lots, all over the place in the back country of Marseilles. This new endeavour became a whole family enterprise. Food and other commodities were rationed. Everything was getting harder and harder to get. My mother, who was in charge of supplies, had to resort to the black market for provisions.

At 6am on Sunday mornings my father and I would set out by tram to its terminus. From there we would walk loaded with vitals for these poor people hidden away from the German and French authorities in the *garrigue* of southern France. Some of these farms were up to eight to ten miles away from the tram, way out in the mountains and it would take us up to five hours of steady walking to reach them. There we would unload the supplies and after a cool drink of water from the well and a quick snack we would be on our way back to the tram. The return trip was always a lot quicker. Of course not all these places were ten miles away from the tram terminals but all had difficult access. Some only had a mule track cut into the side of the mountain to get to them. In one way or another my father managed to keep this dangerous practice alive until the liberation in 1944. After the war he was knighted for his services to humanity.

# 3

# THE GERMAN ARMY
# IN MARSEILLES

## NOVEMBER 1942

On the 11 November 1942, the 'Honourable Armistice', which had been signed between the Vichy Government and the Germans in 1940, was suddenly tossed aside by Hitler. Within a single day the German army took possession of the whole of unoccupied France.

I remember that day very well. I was then fifteen years old. Early on that morning the news had come on the radio that the German forces would enter Marseilles by about midday. My mother in great panic thought it might be safer if we had an extra lock on the front door of the apartment. So she sent me to buy one. Of course, because of the news, every business including hardware shops in Marseilles were closed. For hours I

29

went from one to the other without success. In the end I decided to try the ship chandlers by the port, so there I went. One of them whose owner lived on the premises was open. I got the Yale lock that my mother wanted but by then the Germans had arrived and I couldn't get back. I was stuck on the wrong side of the city. The Germans were pouring in cutting the city in two.

Tanks would set themselves up on the footpaths at various intersections. Their crews dressed in black uniforms would sit on top of the huge machines and smirk at the people. Some trucks would unload machine guns and sandbags in different places and soldiers would immediately man the positions. Trucks, and more tanks and more troops were pouring in. I was anxious to get home; I knew my mother would be worried but I could not cross the streets. The Germans were coming in from everywhere, and even though they did not seem to interfere with the population, in the streets all we could do was stand there and watch them come in.

Later that day I reached the Cours Belzunce. There someone took a shot at the incoming army from a high window in one of the buildings. Of course the Germans immediately retaliated and to this day I don't know what sort of weapon they used but, within minutes, that window became a huge big hole in the façade of the building. I was not near that spot when it happened but I saw it from the distance.

By the time I got home it was nearly dark. My mother was worried sick. She thought that I might have been arrested, dismembered by the Germans, torn to pieces and thrown into the port. But things had not been that bad. After thousands upon thousands of Germans had entered Marseilles and blocked the streets for hours, the population was finally allowed to go about their business and I had managed to go home. My father arrived home shortly after me and verified what I had told my mother.

Within days the situation became as normal as could be expected under German occupation. French flags in official buildings were replaced by those with a swastika on them. On the *Canebiere*, the Capitol cinema became a Soldatenkino, a cinema for German soldiers. At night German squads patrolled the streets. The Gestapo, the German Nazi police, became ardently active in looking for Jews. The food rations were reduced to starvation level. The bread almost black and as solid as a brick, was rationed to a little more than a slice per person per day. Even the food for which ration coupons had been issued was quite often unavailable. A joke of the time was ' To make a sandwich take two bread coupons and put a meat coupon between them.' Of course it wasn't really funny.

It was at about that time that the Resistance started, or at least that is when we became aware that it existed. The Resistance and the *Maquis*. The goal of the Resistance was to obtain information, which could be useful to the Allies and to propagate information which came from England, since the Germans censored all information about the war. The *Maquis* was different. It was the equivalent of the Free French Army in England commanded by General De Gaulle except that it operated within France under direct instructions from England. They wore no uniform, only a blue, white and red armband, the colours of the French flag, with the letters FFI written on it. It meant 'Forces Françaises de l'Interieur.' They were called Terrorists by the newspapers and those French people who still believed in Petain. To fight the *Maquis* the French Government founded a special Corps called the Milice. It was made up of fanatical pro-German young Frenchmen who hated the English and the Jews and had only one ambition, to help Hitler win the war.

At night there was a radio program which came from London. It was called '*Les Français parlent aux Français*'. The French speak to the French. It started with the first bars of Beethoven's 'Fifth Symphony'. It was heavily jammed by the Germans but we used to listen to it. Of course it was forbidden and if you were caught it meant deportation to Germany. It might sound unbelievable now but in those days many were reported to the Germans by their neighbours for having listened to that programme. You could not trust anyone. To reduce the risk of being discovered we used to cover the radio set with several blankets and get under them ourselves to listen to the news from England. It would tell us the true state of the war and would also send several coded messages to the resistance and to the *Maquis*.

Under total German occupation, our Sunday visits to the farms became more dangerous. Nevertheless they still went on. We felt so sorry for these poor devils whose existence depended entirely upon my father's dedication. It must have been very depressing for these poor people, who, in the main had led quite active and rewarding lives, to suddenly find themselves completely isolated from the living world, surviving on charity, without newspapers, radio or electric light. Nothing to do, and all and every day to do it in. Their only human contact limited to the few other unfortunate human beings who shared their miserable isolated existence.

Although they all knew they were in hiding, one day one of the younger men of a group of eight, who were hidden at a farm called Notre Dame des Anges, without telling any of the others where he intended to go, decided to take a walk to the nearest village. We later found out that he wanted to buy sweets. When he got there, walking around the small village asking people in a thick foreign accent where he could buy sweets, which by then were a thing of the past, he was taken to be a German deserter. He was immediately reported to the local police who arrested him. Taken to Marseilles and ferociously questioned by the 'French Gestapo' he told them everything. The next day the place was raided by the Germans, they were all arrested and deported to Germany. None of them survived. Of course that was a risk we all knew existed. We knew all along that if the French or Germans ever discovered those hiding places we would all end up in Germany; but like good old Macbeth, we were, by then, all 'in blood stepped in so far, that going back would have been as tedious as going over.' So we kept carrying on as we had.

By then it was October 1942. Japan had bombed Pearl Harbour, the United States had declared war on Japan and Germany and Italy had declared war on the United States. In Libya and North Africa Rommel and Monty were having a go at each other. In Marseilles, soldiers of the German Afrikacorps were everywhere. Dressed in their yellow uniforms they were waiting to be shipped to the desert. One day, at about 2pm, a bomb went off in the soldatenkino, the Capitol cinema. Many German soldiers were killed. The next day twelve prominent Frenchmen were arrested and executed. The Germans had a list of hostages. It was a list of well to do civilians that they would execute by firing squad every time an attempt was made against any German. It was intended as a deterrent but it did not work as such. Every now and then German patrols would be attacked at night in some of the back streets of Marseilles and the next day hostages would be shot in reprisal.

One day in January 1943 my father was summoned to report to the Prefecture de Marseilles. It was the centre of Government and police headquarters for the region. There he was taken to the office of a man called Sauvanet.

'Mister Nyst, I know that you are hiding Jews, I want to know where they are.' My father just looked at him and said nothing.

'Mr Nyst, if I pick up this telephone you and your family will be deported to Germany tonight.'

My father told us that he remained silent for a while and then told Mr Sauvanet: 'Sir, we all have a conscience, you and I. We both must do what our conscience tells us. Am I under arrest?'

The answer was, 'No, not yet but think about it.'

At school, at about 3pm, I was called to the Principal's office. My father and my brother Phillip were there waiting for me. We said goodbye to the Principal and my father took us home immediately. Phil and I wanted to know what was going on but we were not told until we got home. That evening, Phil, my little brother Edward and I were placed on a train bound for Limoges where, we were told, someone would pick us up at the station. At first it was quite dramatic. Edward was only four years old. Phil and I were quite excited. It was our first time on a train by ourselves. We were alone in the compartment. As the train began to move we started waving frantically to our father and mother through the window. They were waving back following the train along the platform until they could no longer keep up with it. The train started to go faster and faster and suddenly we were alone. Very quickly the excitement faded and soon we were looking at each other trying very hard not to show how scared and desperate we were. Before panic set in I opened a small basket that my mother had given me and we all had dinner. It was a very special picnic of homemade bread, hardboiled eggs, ham and even a tablet of chocolate. After that little feast we all felt a bit more confident and eventually Phil and Doudou, as we called our little brother, fell asleep along the seats. I, of course, had to stay awake.

Before we boarded the train my father had told me, 'Edmond, you are the eldest and you are responsible.' My brothers also had been told to 'Listen to him and do what he says no matter what.' So now here I was, in charge, in a train, at night going to a place called Limoges of which I knew nothing except that I had seen the name written on the back of some of the plates I had used sometimes to set the table for dinner. My instructions were clear: 'Do not fall asleep, the train is only going through Limoges. It stops there and then goes on.' There I was to meet a Mr De Boom, a Dutchman in his mid-sixties. If he was not there when we arrived we were to find a seat and wait until he came. It sounded simple enough.

After four or five hours the conductor came to the compartment and said 'You kids get off in Limoges, it's the next stop in about forty-five minutes.'

# 4

# SAFE IN CONFOLENS

## 1943

By the time the train pulled up at the station we were very excited again. It was the middle of the night. The railway station at Limoges was a huge big place. Even at that time of the night there were quite a number of people on the platform including a lot of armed German soldiers. I started looking around; very few men appeared to be in their mid sixties. I tried eye contact with a few who seemed to be in that age bracket but nothing came of it. I decided to look for a seat but there were none on the platform. As we were about to descend the steps to the tunnel, which led to the main hall a young man in his mid-twenties approached and asked me if we were the Nyst kids. We had been found.

He took Edward's little suitcase, grabbed him by the hand and said 'Follow me.' As it turned out he was the son of the sexagenarian Mr De Boom whom my father had told me would meet us at the station. He was a very friendly young man. I never got to know his other name. I knew he was a Jew and I didn't know whether it was proper to ask a Jew what his Christian name was so I let it go at that. We just called him also Mr De Boom.

The next day, Mr De Boom, the old one, took me aside and told me that they were Jewish. He said that he was returning a favour to my father by getting us out of Marseilles in a hurry but that it was too dangerous for us to live with them. He said that since we were Catholics it would be better for us if we were to live with a French Christian family. He told me that he would see to it, that he knew some very good people and that he would try to arrange it. A few days later he and his son took us to a bus going to a place called Confolens. It wasn't very far from Limoges and the trip was very pleasant. Mr De Boom, his wife and their son were later arrested in January 1944. The three of them died in the gas chambers of Auschwitz.

We arrived in Confolens at about midday. A typical French farmer looking fellow was waving at us even before the bus came to a stop. We had never seen him before and as we looked around in the bus we soon established that there was no doubt that it was us he was waving to. When we got off the bus he rushed to us and gave us each a big kiss and a hug. We were quite surprised and somewhat amused at this ostentatious demonstration of affection. He later told us that it had been for the benefit of some of the other people who had also been waiting for the bus. He was collecting his grandchildren whom he had not seen since before the war. His name was Mercier but he did not tell us then.

After the bus departed and the people dispersed he took us to a house and introduced us to Madame Stivill. She was an autocratic looking woman. Her stern face was crowned with a high forehead. Her hair pulled flat across the rest of her skull was tied in a chignon at the back. She was all dressed in black and looked like an angry schoolmistress. There was nothing there to invite sympathy nor affection. As we kids were eyeing each other in questioning trepidation, Monsieur Mercier and Madame Stivill were having a long whispered conversation at the other end of the corridor. In the end she turned around and said 'Come on you kids, leave your bags there and come and have some lunch.' We were ushered into the kitchen and made to sit at the table. Madame Stivill's three children were already there having their lunch. We were introduced to Claude, the eldest daughter, to Annie and to a four- or five-year-old boy whose name I do not recall.

After lunch we felt more comfortable. There is nothing like a full belly to give you assurance and restore uncluttered perspectives. By then Madame Stivill was asking me about the train trip and Limoges and Marseilles and the Germans. After a while I began to think that my first impression of her might not have been justified. Although her appearance was that of an angry schoolmistress I thought that maybe she was not really as bad as she attempted to look. That maybe, behind this ostentatiously austere presentation, could be a quite normal person. In fact as we later found out she was a nice person and a very nice one at that. After a while she took me to the drawing room away from my brothers and asked me to sit. She told me that she would let my parents know that we had arrived safely. She said that she would keep Edward with her at her place and that Phillip would go with Monsieur Mercier to live in a small village not very far away called Ansac further south on the Vienne River.

I would stay at an inn just outside the town called La Belle Etoile where Mercier would take me on his way to Ansac. She told me that I could come to her place any time to see my little brother Edward and that I could walk to Ansac to see Phillip if I wanted to. Mercier would enrol Phillip at the village school in Ansac and I was to go to the local high school called the College Classique de Confolens. She also said that I could write to my parents but not to post the letters. To give them to her instead and she would see that they be posted from some other town. Just in case they were traced.

After this long conversation she left and sent my brothers in. I was to explain all that to them. It wasn't easy. 'Why can't we stay together?' I wasn't very good at explaining that, probably because inwardly I was asking myself the same question. It seemed definite, things had been arranged and what we wanted did not come into it. Phillip, with a long face, appeared to be somewhat resigned but Edward decided to put on one of his turns. He wasn't going to stay there by himself and 'that was that'. Madame Stivill said 'Leave it to me.' She took us back to the kitchen, we all sat down and began to talk about all sorts of things. After a while Madame Stivill suggested that Annie and her little brother should go out and play outside. 'You too

Edward, you can go out and play with them if you want to.' She did not have to say it twice.

A couple of hours later the three of them were called in for afternoon tea. Edward had made some friends. I noticed that Annie called him Doudou. He had obviously told her that it was his nickname. When I suggested again that he should stay there, at least 'just for tonight' he didn't blow up as I expected him to do and by the time I promised that I would come back to see him the next day he surrendered.

Shortly after that Monsieur Mercier, Phillip and I were on our way. We walked along the bridge across the river and turned left. Mercier was carrying Phil's suitcase and I mine. Within fifteen minutes we arrived at La Belle Etoile. The inn was right on the main road. It was one of those old fashioned inns which had stood by the side of the road for the last three hundred years. It had an uncovered timber lean-to in the front and a large court yard at the left. Being winter there were no tables or chairs outside but through the windows the inside appeared inviting. Creeping up the wall to the top of the lean-to and then to the first floor was the skeletal remains of an avid Virginia Creeper, now, because of winter, totally devoid of leaves.

We went inside and Mercier introduced us to Madame Fumeron and her son Pierre. She was a thick set woman in her early fifties. Plain but with an attractive personality that made her look pretty and that immediately made me feel at home. Pierre was different. In his early twenties he appeared to be very shy and extremely willing to comply. There was no Monsieur Fumeron and Pierre had obviously always been mammy's boy. He was a very good looking young man and he and I later became very good friends.

As the afternoon wore on, Mercier and Phillip departed and I was taken to my room. It was a large room wallpapered with small roses on a pale blue background. A decent size window looked over the lean-to, the road and the Vienne river beyond that. An old antique wardrobe stood against the wall beside the window and on the other side of it was the bed. It was a catafalque sort of edifice. About five feet high with four corner posts which had nothing hanging from them. On the floor, in front of it, was a two step type of stool to enable me to climb on to it. On top was a thick patchwork bed cover and that night I discovered that it had a three foot thick feather mattress.

There was also a porcelain chamber pot under it, and even though the toilet was outside at the back of the courtyard, I never used it. When I got into bed that night I literally sank out of sight. It was claustrophobic. I was sinking in duck feathers. The more I tried to get up the more I went down. It was a losing battle but thankfully before panic set in I fell asleep.

When I woke up the next morning I was soaking wet and so were my top and bottom sheets. Perspiration was simply pouring out of me. With renewed energy I managed to climb out of that bed. The sheets were soaking wet. I didn't know what to do. I didn't want Madame Fumeron to think that I had wet the bed so I took the sheets out and hung them to dry across the front of the big wardrobe.

After that night I just slept on the floor. It was a couple of months before Madame Fumeron discovered my new sleeping habit. Embarrassed, I had to explain. That day while I was at school Pierre replaced the old bed with a different one. I could sleep in it and wake up dry.

The school I went to was the Collège Classique de Confolens. The day after Mercier met us at the bus I went to the College and asked to see the Principal. His name was Monsieur Poilud. He was teaching in class at the time and I was made to wait until the next break. When he saw me, just a kid by himself, asking to be admitted to his school he became suspicious. He wanted to know all about it. I was scared. I thought he might have been a *collaborateur*, a Vichy sympathiser. At first I refused to tell him anything but he insisted. After a while I felt I had to take the risk. Without mentioning my brothers I told him everything. Luckily he wasn't a collaborator, he was one of the few. He told me that he would not enrol me as a student but that I could attend the classes as if I were. He also told me to be careful what I said to some of the other kids because their fathers were for Petain. He also told me not to give my surname to any one and that if at anytime I saw any sign of danger, whether in class or not, to run away.

Within a few weeks life became almost normal again. Phil was at school in Ansac and liked it there, Doudou had definitely accepted his new family and I was a student again. It was not the Jesuits, but I didn't miss them. My parents kept in touch with me by mail and I with them. I even managed to contact my father by telephone one afternoon from Madame Stivill's house.

# 5

# THE WAR IS TAKING SHAPE

## 1943

At the inn we lived well. Madame Fumeron knew a lot of farmers who had supplied her with vegetables and meat before the war and now, even though the food rations were at a starving level, for us at the inn, the dinner table never gave any sign that there was a war on. There was an older man living there with us. He was the only other guest. His name was Koch, Professor Koch. He was a very tall and impressive man in his seventies with long wavy grey hair that started at the middle of his skull and ended well down below his neck. He was a Jew. Before the war he had been a professor of mathematics at the Sorbonne University in Paris. The poor old devil must have been bored stiff all by himself in that inn in Confolens.

43

I suppose that is why, I being a high school student, whenever he got the chance, he would collar me just to discuss different matters with me. It was always very interesting and I enjoyed these discussions very much.

We were not exactly friends but I admired Professor Koch. Sometimes he would give me simple little problems to solve. Like finding the four corners of a square with only a compass, no ruler, and of course I had to prove geometrically that the angles were ninety degrees. He called them very simple little problems. I was sure that they were very simple to him, I found them different. We also used to play a lot of chess. I had been taught to play chess by one of my father's Jewish refugees in Marseilles. In years past he had been the Champion of Belgium, his name was Benjamen Karfiol. He was arrested in forty-one and later was gassed in Auschwitz. His brother Wally had dyed his hair blond and, by selling evening newspapers in front of the German Headquarter in Marseilles, managed to survive the war. The best way to hide is to be right in the middle of them.

One night I discovered that there was someone else living at La Belle Etoile but he was not realistically a guest. He lived in the attic. It was months before I found out. That night, long after I had gone to bed I heard whispers in the passage outside my door. I went to investigate and there, in the middle of the corridor, was a ladder poking through a trap in the ceiling. On it was a man in the process of coming down it and Pierre was there, holding the ladder. When the man reached the floor we were introduced and Pierre explained the mystery man's presence. He did not have to, I had already guessed. His name was also Pierre, he had been arrested a year before by the

Gestapo and had managed to escape. The Fumerons had courageously decided to hide him until the war ended. After more than a year living in darkness in the ceiling the poor fellow was whiter than the sheet of paper I am writing on. Apparently he only came down at night to wash, eat and walk around a little. During the day he slept or lay on a mattress in the attic. No light, he could not even read. This is how it was. The war was taking shape.

One afternoon a truck full of German soldiers pulled up right in front of the College. We all saw it. We were in the yard having a break at the time, and before they even got off the truck I was away. I managed to walk slowly past the truck and then started to run across the bridge away from them. By the time I was half way across, I saw coming towards me, a Citroën car full of *Maquisards*. The windscreen had been taken off and a Bren gun was poking out of it. The car went past me a few metres, stopped and opened fire onto the rear of the German truck. I rushed for one of the pillars in the parapet of the bridge and made myself as small as I could.

When I got a chance to peep, four of the German soldiers were already lying dead on the road at the back of the truck. Then the truck left and turned right. The Citroën followed. A few minutes later, just around the corner from the College, in front of the primary school a big battle started. I was very concerned for my little brother because Madame Stivill's house was right across the road from the College and exactly in front of the four dead German soldiers. The corner where the German truck had fled was an S-bend and by now the shooting was going on out of sight. Apparently the primary school teachers had managed to get the kids out through the back and they were by then lying out of sight on the banks of the Vienne river.

After a while I decided to go to the Stivill's house to see if they were all safe. When I got there the house was empty. Madame Stivill had taken Doudou and her kids out somewhere away from the shooting. I stayed in the house listening to the battle. From time to time I would look out of the window but there was nothing to see. I could hear the firing going on around the corner but I could not see anything. After it got dark the shooting finally stopped and I saw the Citroën getting away back across the bridge. They, we learned later, had lost one man. That night, in retaliation, the Germans set fire to the primary school. We were not allowed to put the fire out, all we were allowed to do was to watch it burn.

One morning, about two weeks after that, Claude Stivill arrived at the inn while I was having breakfast. She was in a deplorable state, out of breath and crying. Madame Fumeron immediately took her aside and tried to appease her. She finally managed to tell us that, early that morning, her father had been arrested by the Gestapo and taken away. Later that day we were told that six other members of the resistance in Confolens had also been arrested. Madame Stivill with Edward and her kids had fled to safety to a place called *Les Quatre Chemins*.

The place was called that because it was a four roads junction. It was about twelve kilometres north east of Confolens. At the junction itself, on one of the corners, was a small *buvette*, literally a place to have a drink. The *buvette* and a large stable were the only buildings there. It was run by a family called

46

Lamant. Monsieur and Madame Lamant were in their late sixties and their unmarried daughter Yvette was about forty-five years old. They and the Stivills were very close friends. They took Madame Stivill and the kids in and there they stayed until things quietened down a little in Confolens. After a couple of weeks Madame Stivill returned to Confolens but my little brother stayed with the Lamants. It was much safer for him there. Particularly since Madame Stivill was now actively scrutinised by the local Vichy authorities.

# 6

# IN THE MAQUIS

## JULY 1943

The 1943 scholastic year ended in July and I was now on holidays. In June I had sat for the Baccalaureat and was waiting for the results. Monsieur Poilud, the Principal of the College, had arranged for me some kind of *nom de plume* for the exam papers which could, he said, be clarified later after the war ended.

Since I had nothing to do, sometimes I would borrow Pierre's bicycle and go to Ansac to see Phillip or ride to *Les Quatre Chemins* to see my little brother. In both places I was always made welcome. I spent a lot more time with Doudou than with Phillip. I felt he needed me more. Sometimes I would even stay the night there with him. That is where I had my first personal contact with the *Maquis*. Yvette Lamant's cousin was in the *Maquis*. Sometimes, at night he would come in with some other *Maquisards* and have a few drinks and a talk at the *buvette*. They were often in contact with London. They would tell us more truthfully how the war was going and what they, themselves, were up to. I was fascinated by their accounts.

A declaration had been passed by the Vichy Government. It was called *La Relève*. It was a preposterous concept connived by the Vichy gang to help the German war effort. The idea was to send to Germany strong healthy young French men to work in German factories so that the German factory workers could be enlisted in the German army. In return Germany would free one French prisoner of war for every man sent by France. This contribution to the German war effort was quite substantial. It freed men to join the army while doing away with having to look after, and feed, French prisoners of war. Not to mention having to look after those who were very sick in German hospitals.

This unconscionable decision by the French Government was actually welcomed by many Petainiste, Petain sympathisers, as we called them. Of course the poor devils who had to go to Germany were not so enthusiastic and many of them then joined the *Maquis* instead. The Milice of course was going out of its way to catch any dissenters. Many were arrested and forced to go. From the beginning of the Vichy era, every foreigner had had to report to the police, show their identity papers and divulge their address. I had no papers, my father had seen to it. I could not even prove my name. Now with the Milice on the rampage I only had two choices left. Either I took another mattress and shared Pierre's sordid existence in the attic at La Belle Etoile or join the *Maquis*.

So one morning I walked all the way to *Les Quatre Chemins* and went to see old Monsieur Lamant. I told him what I had decided to do and to my great surprise he agreed. He also thought that it was the right decision. He told me that he would talk to his nephew next time he saw him and he would let me know as soon as it was arranged. I went back to Confolens to wait. Four days later Yvette came over on her bicycle and told me to be at the *buvette* early Sunday morning.

I was there all right. To make sure, I went there Saturday and spent the night with my brother Doudou. Sunday morning at about ten thirty a large truck pulled up outside the *buvette*. Yvette's cousin and three other *Maquisards* came in. The name he used was Bernard and he asked me if I had my things. I did, I had my suitcase full of clothes and all my books. He told me to take only a change of clothes and to leave the rest there with the Lamants. I did as I was told and we left. We drove for only about half an hour and we arrived at the camp.

It was an old derelict farmhouse. A two storey stone building that was quite dilapidated. Most of the windows were just holes in the façade. On the right at right angles to it was a huge barn also made of stones. It had two large doors open in front of it and by the look of them they had been open a long time and they were open to stay. The side that I could see had no windows. It had obviously been a stable. In front of the two buildings where the truck had pulled up was a very big open space with two large chestnut trees on the opposite side of the barn. Under the trees were some long farm tables and seats where a number of men were eating. Bernard told me to go to the stable, find myself a spot, leave my things there and come back. It was lunch-time.

In the stable I found myself a spot unoccupied near the back wall. I dragged some straw from a trough and made myself a cosy little nook. I left my things there and went out. When I got back to the table Bernard had brought me an FFI arm band and a huge bowl of bean soup thickened with huge big pieces of pork. I cut myself a large slice of bread from a three foot round loaf which was on the table and had a very good meal. I was hungry and I was enjoying all this when a motorbike arrived. The rider walked to the farm house and went inside.

Within minutes he came out again with another man and they both walked towards us at the tables. The other man said that something was on and to get ready. Bernard introduced me to him. He shook my hand and told me not to tell him my name. He said 'Just call me Bob and from now on your name is Pierre' I wasn't given a choice. I kind of laughed. I thought that Pierre must have been a very popular name in this part of France. He asked one of the men to fetch him a Sten Gun and when he got it he asked me if I had ever seen one of these? I told him no.

He said, 'It's very simple, this is how it works. You put the magazine in there …' and he did it … 'Then you see this little switch? If you push it this way it fires one shot at a time. Look …' and he fired five or six bullets into the open field behind us. Then he said, 'This way it's rapid firing see?' and he fired a volley in the same direction.

'OK? That's yours,' he said and he handed me the gun. 'Keep it clean. The boys will show you how to recharge the magazine.' And that was the full extent of my *Maquis*' military training. A few minutes later two big trucks came out of nowhere and we all climbed aboard. I was terribly excited. I was in it at last. My own gun. A Sten Gun, which fired real bullets. All I had to do now was to find myself some Germans. I was sixteen years and eight months old.

As we got on our way one of the men in the truck gave me another magazine for the Sten gun. It had no bullets in it, it was empty. On the floor were three crates of ammunition, one of them was open and some of the men were charging their spare magazines. I only had two but some of them had three or four. I watched them recharge their magazines for a few minutes and then did the same. I did not have to be shown. I filled the magazine that I had been given with the nine-millimetre bullets from the open crate. Acting as professionally as I could, know-it-all me did it as if I had done it all my life. I don't think that I impressed anyone but I was pleased with myself. We drove for several hours and by the time we got there, which seemed to be nowhere, it was almost dark.

Some *Maquisards* from another group were already there. They were in the process of laying big and heavy horse drawn ploughs across the road and tying them together with chains. I had no idea what it was all about but since I was expected to know I did not want to ask. I had to lend a hand also and by the time we were finished we had laid a spectacular metal barrage across the road all safely bound together with chains. I, and a dozen or so other men, were told to take position in the ditch alongside the road and stop the German convoy if it came this way.

All the others left with the trucks to erect similar barrages on other roads in the area. We were told that a German supply convoy was due but they didn't know which way it would come, so we were blocking all the roads.

I was good at mathematics but I did not have to waste my talents to estimate the odds of the situation we were in. Interpreting the semantic meaning of the word 'convoy' on the one side and us, a small bunch of only twelve or fifteen men on the other side, I very quickly came to the conclusion that if the convoy ever came this way, even with the ploughs chained tightly together across the road, our chance of ever having another drink at the *buvette* at *Les Quatre Chemins* was very slim indeed. I for one only had two magazines, the one in the gun and the one I recharged in the truck. Not quite sixty bullets in all. I didn't know what the others had but we had not been left with extra ammunition.

That night we had no dinner. We waited but did not talk. Later it was decided that one of us should take position somewhere near the barrage and keep watch while the others would try to sleep for a while. My turn came at about 2am. I walked over to where I knew the ploughs were and hid behind a tree. The sky was covered by clouds and it was pitch black. I sat at the base of the tree and fought hard to keep awake. Suddenly I heard something. I lay down flat on the ground behind the tree and looked out. I could not see anything. There I lay for a while and then I heard it again. It was a noise of chains being moved.

I could not see the barrage but the noise definitely came from there. I waited and there it came again, chains, definitely chains and it came from where I knew the barrage was. I was too scared to move forward to the barrage to have a closer look but the sound was definitely chains and it came from there. After about ten or fifteen minutes of this I realised that some Germans were undoing the chains in order to clear the road for the convoy. So I fired. A whole magazine in rapid firing. Within seconds the others came and took position around where I was. The chain noise had stopped. They asked me why I fired and I told them. We didn't know what to do. Eventually we walked over to the barrage. It was still there neatly tied up with chains. So we resumed the night schedule and waited for dawn. At daylight, behind the fence on the other side of the road was a dead cow. It had been shot. It had a chain around its neck. That chain was about five feet long and at the other end of it was tied a large lump of wood to stop it from running when someone wanted to milk her.

We were there for ten days waiting for the convoy. Twice a day someone would bring a large copper saucepan of bean soup with pork, a demijohn of cider, bread and packets of tobacco and paper to roll cigarettes. That is when I started to smoke. The convoy never came, at least not our way. During my watches I never heard anymore chains being moved and I did not shoot anymore cows. That waiting period of course fermented a lot of jokes about Pierre's vigilance. 'Be careful when you pull your watch out of your pocket, you might get shot'. Or, 'I wouldn't keep my watch on that chain if I were you, it's too dangerous, your life depends on it. Haa Haa Haa'. Of course that was only within our small group by the barrage. When we got back to the farm the full story really erupted. The jokes multiplied until Bob, who was in charge, said that it could very well have been the Germans clearing the road and that, had he been there himself, he would have done the same thing. After that things quietened down a lot.

Life in the *Maquis* was either very exciting or very dull. When nothing was on we just did nothing. Most of the men played cards, smoked and drank cider. This was in Charente, a part of France where they eat haricot beans and drink cider. In the old farm house, right by the entrance was the kitchen. It did not look like a kitchen. It had a sink on one side against a wall and a bench beside it. On the opposite wall was a huge fireplace. Inside hung a large cast iron bucket, almost the size of a bath tub. In it, I discovered, was cooking the perennial haricot beans and pork soup. Every morning the cook would throw more beans and more pork into it and added water and salt. The bath tub was never taken off the hook and the fire under it never went out. We just dug into it whenever we were hungry.

One afternoon Bob called me and told me to have dinner early that night. 'You're coming with us,' he said. I knew I was not supposed to ask where so I just said 'OK'. As night fell and the evening dragged on I thought that maybe he had forgotten all about it. At about 10pm a truck arrived and that was it. About a dozen of us climbed aboard and we left. We did not go very far but it took over an hour to get there. It was night time, we did not use headlights and the road through the woods was only a track. Finally we stopped at a large clearing.

We couldn't see much but Bob knew what had to be done. We built three stacks of firewood in a straight line. These stacks were about one hundred metres apart. Beside each of them was placed a can with kerosene in it. Later three men were detached to stand by them. I and the other men were sent back to the woods around the clearing to keep watch in case a German patrol came. We waited there for hours. It was cold and nothing was happening. Then I heard one of the men say, 'I think I hear it.' We all paid attention and within a minute or so we definitely heard it. A plane was coming. Bob was in the middle of the clearing and with a torch was sending some kind of signal which I couldn't see. Then before we saw the plane we saw some lights flashing in the sky and at the same time the three stacks of wood came alight. The plane made two passes and disappeared. The fires were immediately put out and we half saw and half guessed the parachutes coming down.

The truck came back into the clearing and we all went in to help. Each parachute had a metal container attached to it. These containers were round cylinders, a little over two feet (about half a metre) in diameter and about eight feet (about 2.5 metre) long. They were painted khaki. At the base, that part which first comes in contact with the ground, was a contraption made to collapse. It looked like two woks welded together face to face. It was there to reduce the parachute impact with the ground and protect any fragile items inside the container. That night we received eight containers, which apparently was quite a lot. They were all over the place and we had to find them in the dark. The light coloured parachutes attached to them made it somewhat easier. Some of the containers were very heavy and it took five or six men to load them on the truck. By the time we had loaded all the containers and the silk parachutes it was almost daylight.

The return trip to the farm in daylight was a lot quicker. When we got there we all went to the kitchen for breakfast.

Haricot bean soup with pork. It was not bacon and eggs with toast and marmalade but it was delicious. At that age, when you are hungry, anything you eat is delicious. By the way, I don't know about now, but in those days, haricot beans was the staff of life in Charente. In their dialect they call them *mangetta*. It was on every table, in every home, at every meal every day. And it was certainly the same in the *Maquis*.

By the time we had our breakfast the men had unloaded the containers and were opening them. Inside were a lot of goodies. Sten guns, spare magazines, nine-millimetre ammunition and lots and lots of explosives. Little greasy dark grey cardboard boxes full of soft TNT. There were also small tin boxes of detonators neatly packed in sawdust and many rolls of fuse. In one of the containers we found six Bren guns. That was new, we didn't have any before that. They looked like some kind of rifle with a folding biped at the front. They fired .303 bullets from a curved magazine, which held twenty-eight cartridges. They could fire single shots or rapid firing, like a machine gun. With each of them came two spare barrels. When using rapid firing for a while the barrel would get very hot and had then to be replaced. It only took three seconds to do that. In the same container were also a number of Smith & Wesson revolvers together with their pouches and belts made of thick webbing type material. In some containers, packed between the various items, were soldiers' uniforms. English battledress. One container only had ammunition in it. In another container we found three crates of hand grenades and a few magnetised time bombs. They were not exactly bombs, they were small rectangular type packages with a time fuse in them which could be pre-set and a magnet by which it could be stuck to any metal part of a vehicle.

One morning, a few days later just before lunch, a messenger arrived and it was on again. We got on the trucks and we left. It must have been quite far from the farm because it was mid afternoon by the time we got there. 'There' was a road lined with tall trees on both sides. It was at the top of a small rise in a cutting about four feet (about 1.2 metre) down from the surrounding ground. As soon as we arrived we were told to take position in the fields on both sides of the road. Some of the men were told to get some trees down across the road. Following orders they blew down about a dozen trees from each side of it with TNT and came to join us.

I don't know what the field on the other side of the road was but the one I was in had been wheat and the wheat had been harvested. The stubble was only about five inches (about 12.7 centimetres) high; a size which made it very difficult for one to conceal oneself behind. At first we were all lying down flat. As flat as we could make ourselves be. After an hour or so I and some of the others decided to sit up. Obviously we were waiting for the Germans but they weren't coming. Later still we stood up and started to chat.

Night fell and we were still there. It was getting cold and we had not had anything to eat or drink since breakfast. In the middle of the night a couple of fellows came over and we were given a large slice of bread and a hunk of cheese. We also got a long drink of cider out of the demijohn. That made us feel better. We didn't mind dying, but if we had to, we wanted it to be with a full stomach.

It was in the early hours of the morning, long before daylight, we were all standing up flapping our bodies with our arms trying to keep warm when we heard the convoy coming. In less than a second we were all flat on the ground again. The German trucks stopped where the trees were blocking the road. One truck remained there while the others began to reverse. We could hear them sawing the logs with two-men saws. There were no chain saws in those days. All of a sudden the shooting started. I don't know who fired the first shot but I am pretty sure it was one of us. With the road in the cutting the Germans had a much better position than us. They were like in a trench, protected by solid ground, all we had was five inches of wheat stubble to hide behind. And it was not bullet proof. The moon kept coming on and off from behind the clouds but still luckily it was night-time. When it was shining the Germans had a good view of us, all we could see was the top of their trucks.

The shooting was pretty hectic for a while then it died out somewhat. It was still going on, but we could hear the Germans cutting the trees and the truck dragging them away. I was about fifty to seventy metres from the cutting. At that distance the Sten Gun is not very accurate. We didn't seem to be doing much damage. Suddenly all hell broke loose. The Germans had rigged up a couple of heavy machine guns on top of the cutting and they were firing at ground level. I could hear many of our fellows being hit and screaming and then someone shouted in French to pull back. Some stood up and started to run. They were immediately shot. I decided to crawl backwards, which in stiff stubble is almost impossible. I did however manage to put some more distance between me and the Germans.

By then it was almost daylight and I thought when the sun comes up this is going to turn into a real turkey shoot. The Germans had been working non stop to clear the road. During the night one of our men had crawled close to them and had thrown two hand grenades. He was killed immediately. We all saw it, he didn't have a chance. By then we were not shooting anymore, there was obviously no point to it. The Germans were still shooting but the firing was more erratic. Then suddenly the truck that had been dragging the trees went through, they had cleared the road. The machine guns were still firing while the rest of the convoy followed. The last truck picked them up and they went. We had not had a chance to actually attack the convoy. We should have been positioned further down the road where the trucks had reversed to but we had not. We had been told to take position in that field of stubble and it had been a disaster. Those of us who could stand up did. We walked over to those who didn't stand up. Most of them were dead. We lost eight men that night. When I say men, I was not yet seventeen years old and most of the 'men' were under twenty two.

That morning was a very miserable one. Completely devoid of the usual bragging, laughing and jockeying. We didn't speak. We started to pick up the dead. We had no stretchers to carry them. Four of us would pick up a limb each and walk to the trucks with the dead guy. We laid them all down behind the cab of one of the trucks. Except for the one who had thrown the grenades all the others had all been shot either in the head or on top of the shoulders. There wasn't much blood. Two men had been wounded, both in the legs. Not badly, only flesh wounds but they were bleeding a lot. Bob had some first aid bandages and he fixed them up as best as he could. We had no doctors, not even medics. I knew that we had received first aid kits by parachute but we had never been issued with them.

By the time we got back to the farm it was almost lunch time. I went to the kitchen and had a plate of soup. When I came out the truck with the dead men had gone. They were always taken away very quickly to be buried. It was done by others who were not members of the *Maquis*. I didn't know any of them, I think they were members of the resistance and I was told that there was also a priest involved.

# 7

# SUPPLY TRAIN ATTACKED

## CHRISTMAS 1943

I was only a bit of a kid but I soon realised that we were very badly organised. After the episode with the ploughs across the road and twelve men only to stop a full convoy; and the fiasco we had just witnessed, where we gave the enemy the advantaged position in the cutting and where we were given orders to lay down in an open field, I began to question the experience and the wisdom of our leaders. Bob was one of them. I never got to know his real name. He was a very nice guy with a lot of guts but he had never been a soldier. He had originally organised a bunch of men to fight for De Gaulle and had been voted their leader by them. There had never been any military training.

It worked this way. The leader of seven or eight men would call himself a corporal, when he had twelve or fifteen men he would then be a sergeant. By the time a hundred or so men had joined the group he would be a captain or a major. Without at any time ever having opened a simple manual on military tactics. We fought with courage and devotion and survived with luck. We were all pretty much aware of this desperate situation but no one was prepared to talk about it. It would have sounded as if we were scared, so we just kept putting our lives on the line and hoped for the best.

One day, straight after lunch we boarded the trucks again. We drove the whole afternoon and at dusk we left the road and pulled up in the woods alongside of it. There we had to wait until dark. It was winter and by half past five it was pitch dark. We left the trucks and walked a few hundred metres to a railway line. I didn't know exactly where we were but I knew that we were somewhere near Limoges. The line was on a bend on top of a fifteen foot (about 4.5 metres) high embankment. With huge big T-shaped socket spanners we set out to unscrew the rails. They were held down on to the sleepers with six inch long screws with an hexagonal head. We unscrewed about three lengths of rail on the external side of the bend. Being on a bend the rails sprang back a little but by and large they still appeared as if they were still in position except that now they were loose. We took positions for quite a distance along the railway line and waited. Some of us were concerned for the engine driver and the fireman. We knew they would be French and doing their job but we were told not to think about them. We were told to think about a train full of supplies for the German army and guarded by German soldiers.

In the early hours of the morning we heard the train coming. We were waiting for it and we were ready. As it approached the bend, the driver must have noticed that the rails did not quite line up and applied the brakes. Of course it was too late. The engine and three or four wagons derailed and rolled over down the embankment. The other wagons also derailed but they stayed on top. It was a supply train with only a few dozen German soldiers as guards. When the commotion came to a stop we saw the soldiers jump down from the wagons and we opened fire. They returned only with rifle fire. This time we were in a command position. We had trees to take cover behind and we could see them better than they could see us. We hit a few of them, wounded or dead we had no idea.

After about fifteen minutes the Germans stopped firing and so did we. We cautiously climbed up the embankment to that portion of the train which had not rolled off the bank. There were no Germans there any more, neither alive, wounded or dead. They seemed to have run away on the other side of the railway line taking their casualties with them. We got onto the wagons and began destroying everything on them. They were mostly the table top type wagons but some had low side rails. There were a few wooden crates here and there but the rest were mostly staff cars with heavy cannons hitched to them and a lot of German jeeps.

At first we were using hand grenades without much effect. We tried to set fire to them but that did not work either so we decided to use explosives. It was more effective but slow. In those days there were no electric impulse firing boxes, we had to light the fuses with matches. Some of the jeeps, and a few of the staff cars had fallen off the train when it derailed. We blew them up also. The TNT was very effective on the vehicles but not on the cannons. One fellow squashed a packet of TNT so that it would fit inside the barrel of one of the cannons and set it off. It was a waste of time. It made a lot of noise and nothing else. Some of the boys had picked up a couple of German antitank guns, they were small ones, they looked like toys on small solid rubber wheels. Later we blew them up too because we could not find any ammunition for them and we did not want to stick around too long looking for it. That morning we all came back safely. Later we were told that the engine driver was OK but that the fireman had been badly hurt.

And so, a couple of weeks after that, Christmas came and went and the new year brought us into 1944. The festivities had been heralded with a lot of cider, a lot of *gnole*, the farm-made brandy, and a lot of roasted chestnuts. But the main menu had still been haricot bean soup with pork.

Early in the new year things became a lot more hectic. Because of the activities of the different *Maquis* throughout France, the Germans decided to really do something about it. They were now determined to wipe us all out once and for all. Whereas up until then we had been looking for them, they were now looking for us. Aided with the French Milice they really got stuck into the different groups of *Maquis*. The one in the Alps, the *Maquis* of the Vercors was completely wiped out.

We, at the farm, were attacked one morning by a company of the Milice. We fought from just before daylight until well after dark when some of us managed to run away. It would be nicer if I could say that we retreated but it would not be the truth, we just ran for our lives. We lost about a third of our men, either killed or taken by the Milice, which, in reality, meant the same thing. Neither the Germans nor the Milice took us as prisoners. Whenever they captured one of us alive he was immediately shot dead by the side of the road. In retaliation we did the same thing, we took no prisoners. After Eisenhower landed in North Africa, he had made a proclamation to the Germans that if caught we were to be treated as prisoners of war. The Germans never abided by it so neither did we.

Somehow we managed to regroup the next day . There were only forty or forty five of us left. We were a quite dilapidated and miserable looking bunch. We were tired, cold and hungry. We had lost everything. All we had were the weapons we had in our hands and the few ammunitions that only some of us still had. All the materials that we had received by parachute were now in the hands of the enemy. We knew that the Germans and the Milice would be sending out patrols to look for us but we could not engage them, we had no ammunition. The only thing left for us to do was to get away as fast and as far as possible. We could hardly stand but we started to walk and it began to snow. Bob seemed to know where he was taking us. We had no idea where we were going and we were too pissed off just even to ask, we just followed. We walked through woods and along hedges, we crossed brooks and roads and by nightfall we reached a forest. There we stopped and sat down as best we could. It was still snowing. We were told not to light fires.

We were miserably cold and hungry but no one complained. Thinking of the fellows we had left at the farm made us realise how well off we all really were. Later that evening a bunch of men came. We didn't know them. They brought some of these three foot round breads, large round cheeses, several demijohns of cider and a few bottles of *gnole*. They also brought some canvas tarpaulins to make tents with. We first got stuck into the food and the drinks and miraculously the morale went up a bit. Some wisecracks could be heard from the fellows who were trying to set up tents with the tarpaulins. They didn't seem to be getting anywhere. In the end they gave up.

We were asked to collect dead leaves to make bedding. Later the tarpaulins were laid over the leaves and doubled up. That night we slept sandwiched in the tarpaulins, about a dozen of us lying side by side with our weapons between us. Even our heads were covered up. The men on guard duty had laid small branches and leaves over the top of the tarpaulin to keep the snow from falling directly on top of us. From time to time, during the night, they would lift up the top of the tarpaulin to freshen the air underneath. That evening I went out like a light and slept all night. I wasn't wakened to stand guard.

When I got up it wasn't snowing anymore but we were in thick fog. Most of the men were already up and drinking coffee brought by the same men who had brought the food and the tarpaulins the night before. There were two huge galvanised milk buckets full of it. They had brought more bread as well and the men were cutting thick slices of it and dipping them in their coffee. A typical French way to breakfast. I could never come at that. The men who had brought the coffee and the bread were not *Maquisards*. They were old men, *Maquis* sympathisers, all in their mid sixties. One of them had a farm nearby and apparently Bob knew him. The others were simply there to help.

By then I had been issued with a rifle. It was a hell of a lot more accurate than the Sten Gun. With it I could hit a target nine hundred yards away (about eight hundred metres). It was an English army rifle; a .303 Royal Enfield. The cartridges came in small clips of five contained in a cloth bandolier, which we could carry over our shoulders and throw away when empty. The rifle had a magazine holding ten cartridges. To load it, all one had to do was to open the bolt, place the clips on top of the bridge and press the cartridges into the magazine with the thumb. Done twice and it was fully loaded. It was only a bolt action single shot rifle but with some experience we could manage to fire a bullet per second if we had to.

Only those of us who had proved to be 'good shots' were issued with the rifles. The others still had the Sten Guns. Some of the men, given a choice, still preferred the Sten Guns. They felt that its rapid firing capability gave them better protection. I certainly didn't, I liked my rifle. It was only later, when I was given a Bren gun that I benefited from both, the precision of single shot firing and the accuracy of long distance rapid fire. With the Bren came an assistant to insert a new magazine when empty and change the barrel when it got too hot.

This life in the open air went on for some time. We had no supplies and could not do anything. The haricot bean and pork soup resumed the following day with disastrous consequences at night under the tarpaulins.

The stench at times was unbearable but since we all contributed we could hardly complain.

The day came when we moved again. This time it was to the Chateau. In French it means castle. It wasn't a castle with a moat, ramparts and towers, it was, or rather had been, a three-storey stately residence on top of a hill with a lot of open ground around it. I said had been, because now the roof and most of the top floor were in ruins. It had, obviously, been lived in until the war began. There was still quite a lot of furniture and a few beds there. I didn't score one. I had to go nearly a mile to a haystack to get myself something soft to sleep on. It took me the whole day to settle myself in but at last I was comfortable. I had got myself a spot against a wall in a large room on the ground floor. The kitchen wasn't very far away and it was nice and warm.

Not far from the chateau, but out of sight, was a barn cum machinery shed. We didn't use it because if attacked we stood a better chance to defend ourselves at the chateau with the open ground around it. One day poking around in the barn, under a hessian bag, I found a small motorbike. It was an old Peugeot with flat tires and shrouded in cobwebs. There was a hand pump still hooked to the frame. When I started to pump the tires they came up. It had a magneto and a kick starter which gave a spark. But of course there was no petrol around so I could not try it. I replaced the bag and forgot about it.

By then we had been re-supplied with ammunition and explosives. Not by parachute, but from another *Maquis* nearby. Each one of us also had received a brand new pair of boots. They were fancy mountain boots that another *Maquis* group had found on a German supply train that they had hijacked. We were told they came from Spain. The train had been full of them. They had been meant for the German soldiers on the Russian front but now they were in our hands.

As time went on we gradually resumed our activities against the Germans without too many losses. The war in Italy was going well. The Italians had surrendered and the Germans had been kicked out of Monte Cassino. By now it looked as if the Allies indeed had a chance to win the war. The 'miserable few' from 1940 were now increasing in numbers, in spite of the terrible reprisals by the Germans for the actions of the *Maquis*. Whenever any aggression was made against the Germans they would retaliate against the civilian population. They would execute twenty or thirty men at random every time we did something to them. I did feel very bad about it and even, at times, began to wonder if the incursions we did on the Germans were so valuable to the Allied cause to warrant such atrocities in retaliation. The general consensus was, we have a job to do and we're doing it. Without telling anyone I did not feel easy about it.

I was always an early riser. Very early one morning a man arrived on a motorcycle. It was Bernard, I thought he had been killed at the farm for I had not seen him since that day. He was in a hurry, he had an urgent message for Bob but in passing me he said, 'They've landed.' I didn't know what he meant. He was going so fast, I could not ask him what he was talking about. Within minutes we all knew; Bob came out and told us. The Allies had landed in Normandy.

'How is it going?'

'We don't know yet.'

'What are we supposed to do?'

'I don't know, we'll have to wait for orders.'

Bernard had left, he was now an *estafette*, a messenger rider.

Within an hour or so he was back. This time he had instructions for Bob. 'Too early to tell but they have established a front, some are already moving inland, some are still stuck on the beach.' It was 6 June 1944.

Our orders were to stop all German transports going north. Parachute supply would intensify. If we were to be of any help supply certainly had to intensify. We were nearly out of ammunition again and badly in need of heavier weapons.

A few days later we were satisfied. That night I was again on parachute duty and we received what we wanted. We only got four containers but in them was what we needed; plenty of ammunition plus Bazookas, Pita guns, and some two-inch mortars. All these weapons were new to us. We found 'How to use' notes inside the containers, both in French and in English. This is when Bob realised that I could read and speak English and with that qualification I was immediately promoted to sergeant. I did not have stripes to wear on my arms but the word was passed around and they all knew that Pierre was now a sergeant.

The Bazooka was a very simple weapon. It was a tube about six feet (about 1.8 metre) long and about three inches (about 7.5 centimetres) in diameter. Half way was a wooden grip and a trigger. At the back end of it were two electric wires about a foot long hanging down. In the wooden grip was a small torch battery. The ammunition was a small rocket about eighteen inches (about 45 centimetres) in length. To fire it the rocket was inserted into the rear end of the tube by an assistant, the two wires were then connected to the terminals on the rocket and the pulling of the trigger would fire it. The rocket produced a dangerous, long flame at the back of the weapon before it left the tube. It had a fairly accurate range of up to about three hundred yards (about 280 metres). It was not effective against tanks but it was very much so against trucks full of soldiers.

The Pita, on the other hand, was a real antitank weapon. It fired a funny looking bomb. The explosive part of it was almost round like a ball. At the front end of it, it had a pointed sort of tube which probably worked like an acetylene torch to penetrate armour plates and at the other end it had a thicker tube which was fitted with directional fins. The overall shape of the projectile was somewhat like the body of a wasp. We did not use the Pitas often because it had an atrocious recoil. Enough to put your shoulder out of joint. One could not fire it standing up. Even lying down one had to have one's feet against the base of a tree to survive the impact. They had an effective range of about seventy yards (about 64 metres)

The two-inch mortars on the other hand were very popular; unfortunately we only had three of them. They were painted yellow. They had a barrel about two feet (about half a metre) long and a narrow, folding base plate. The bomb would be inserted from the top and detonated when required with a round handle on the side at the bottom of the barrel. Their effective range was not spectacular but used properly they were capable of very satisfactory results.

# 8

# AN ESCAPADE ON BRANDY

## 1944

The landing in Normandy had been successful and the Allies were getting close to Paris. When there was nothing on we were always bored. We didn't know how to occupy ourselves. I kept walking around the place. I could not understand why this chateau we were in, which must have been a substantial edifice, did not have a cellar. Normally such a prestigious residence as this one once had been would have had an extensive basement. Maybe we hadn't found it.

One afternoon, with a friend of mine called Claude, we decided to investigate. Under the main flight of stairs going up was a cupboard with a door. We knew that it was full of rubbish but I surmised that if the chateau had a basement, that would be the logical access to it. I was right. After removing old suitcases and cardboard boxes and old picture frames and all sorts of other rubbish, we saw the stairs going down.

With great expectations of wealth we descended. The basement was empty. All there was there were two very large 50-litre demijohns. They were both full. Their corks had been sealed with red candle wax. We uncorked one of them and from the smell we discovered that it was *gnole*. I had a sip of it and it nearly dissolved my teeth. It was undrinkable. Claude struck a match and read a small cardboard label attached to the neck of the demijohn. It was a date: '1865'. The one next to it which I had tasted read 1863. We could not bring them up. The straw type packing around them had two handles but after all this time they were just about rotten, we weren't game to try them.

Claude went upstairs and got a jug. We dispensed some liquid around to the boys but they all thought that we were trying to kill them. As a joke I emptied some of it on a plate and struck a match to it. We were all laughing when I thought of the old motorbike in the barn. Suddenly, there we were, Claude and I walking to the barn, me with a jug of *gnole* in my hand.

I poured the *gnole* in the fuel tank and kicked the starter several times but nothing happened. The spark was good but the engine wouldn't even cough. Claude and I had planned an escapade to *Les Quatre Chemins* and Confolens. I wanted to see my brother and he wanted to go to say hullo to his parents.

He had found an old bicycle somewhere, a girl's bicycle, but Confolens was too far. We could not be away from the chateau too long in case something came up. I decided to try a rolling start.

From the barn, the track to the main road was down hill for a couple of miles. The motorbike was very small and only had one seat. I would have to tow Claude on his bicycle with a rope. The idea was to try to start the bike rolling down the hill; if it didn't start we would leave it there and walk back to the Chateau. We both went. The rolling was good. I put the bike into gear and released the clutch. For a long time nothing happened. I was about to stop and ditch the bike when there was an explosion. A large cloud of light grey smoke came out of the exhaust pipe and the engine started. We couldn't believe it. Claude came up on his bike, grabbed the towing rope with one hand and gripping the handle bar with the other, we were on our way.

We were not going fast but it was still faster than riding a bike. From time to time, Claude would shout to me that the exhaust fumes were making him drunk, but he never did let go of the rope. After a while he acquired a taste for it and indeed enjoyed the fumes.

At *Les Quatre Chemins*, I saw my little brother who was very pleased to see me. Old Monsieur Lamant told me that *Maquis* trucks went past their place very often. And that Edward, who was now six years old, would run out of the house every time he heard a truck coming and would wave a small French flag at them. One day, however, the truck had been a German one and Edward had been waving the French flag at the enemy, having noticed too late that they were Germans. He had run away to hide at the bottom of the paddock. No drastic consequences ensued from this childish exuberance. After that, apparently, his patriotism was a little more subdued and contained.

Yvette gave us some rolled pancakes filled with her special pork rillette to eat and we drank some cider. I didn't want to stay long. I couldn't let the motorbike get cold or I wouldn't have been able to start it again. And soon we were on our way to Confolens, towing Claude on the bicycle. I couldn't go fast; still forty five minutes later we were having coffee at Claude's place. His father, though glad to see his son, was irate that we had come all this way by ourselves. He thought it was stupid and dangerous. Although we did not wear our FFI armbands and had no weapons with us we were wearing the fancy boots destined for the Russian front and that was a sure give away. The old fellow was right of course but at the time I did not agree with him.

We wanted to be back before dark but we had stayed too long and now the bike was cold. I tried to kick-start it many times but nothing happened. We were stuck there in front of Claude's parents' house. Attracted by the commotion the neighbours were now coming out of their houses. Some were offering their mechanical expertise to help me start it but when I told them the reason why the bike wouldn't kick-start they all started to laugh their heads off. They took turns pushing me up and down the street to roller start the bike but it did not seem to work. In the end, after a lot of pushing, success. Of course they all came over to have a smell of the exhaust and Claude and I left them laughing. When we arrived back at the chateau Bob got onto us. We had gone without permission and without telling anyone. He told us how stupid we had been and ordered us never to do it again. He explained that we were badly needed even if we had nothing to do. That kind of logic, of course, is difficult to accept when you are seventeen years old but we never did it again.

Since the Allies had landed in Normandy, various *Maquis* had taken it upon themselves to 'liberate' various towns from the Germans. I was quite sure that no instruction for such individual initiative had ever come from England. Our orders from there had been to impede the Germans in their activities. What some of the *Maquis* were doing was noble but foolish. They would enter a town, attack the German garrisons; either kill or take them prisoner and take over the running of the town; city hall, post office, telephones and all. It was a great morale booster for the *Maquis* and for the population. Alas, it didn't always work. In some instances the Germans would want their town back.

A few days after the Normandy landing, the *Maquis* from Coreze decided to liberate the town of Tulle. It was a fairly large town and after a fierce battle the *Maquis* did take it over. The German soldiers still alive were taken prisoner and the town was free in the hands of the *Maquis*. The Germans however did not intend to leave it at that. A couple of days later they came back. This time with tanks. The *Maquis* could not hold them back, and after a courageous battle they had to withdraw. The population unfortunately was left behind.

On the afternoon of 9 June 1944 the Germans tied a noose to every lamp post, tree and balcony rail in the main street of the town. They then entered the houses and took out chairs and stools. Then they went around the town and arrested ninety-nine men, all civilians These men were taken back to the main street where the nooses awaited them. They were made to climb on the chairs and tie the nooses around their own necks. One of the soldiers would then kick the chairs from under their feet and there they hung. The youngest one to die was not quite seventeen.

In front of the Tivoli bar they had set up a loud speaker belting out music to cover the screaming of the victims. As if this had not been enough, that night one hundred more civilians were arrested and deported to Germany. None of them ever came back. It was certainly a horrible price to pay for a few days liberation when the real thing was coming anyway at no cost at all to the civilians.

Later that day of course we got the news, and that night we discussed it amongst ourselves; the military worth of the actions of the *Maquis* against the Germans, and the appalling consequences on the civilian population. A few, and I was one of them, were wondering if it was really worth it. Were we in fact shortening the war at the cost of terrible reprisals? We few doubted it. The others of course vehemently discarded out of hand the comparison. 'It's war', they would say without any further thought.

The very next day we heard about Oradour. By then I had been issued with a Bren gun and a young fellow had been assigned as my assistant. He was new and came from North-Eastern France, Alsace or Lorraine, I am not quite sure, near the German border. I can't remember his name, I am not even sure that I was told what his name was. Anyway he didn't last long, he was killed within a few days.

That day, 12th June, Bob asked me to go with him. He told me to bring the Bren and a couple of extra magazines. We got into a Citroën car. There were four of us: Bob, a lieutenant called Guy, a driver and me. The car had no windscreen and I sat in the front beside the driver with the Bren sticking out over the bonnet of the car. We were going to Oradour sur Glane.

Oradour was a small town, about twenty kilometres from Confolens. Early on Saturday afternoon, 10 June 1944, only a few days after the Normandy landing a company of German SS troops led by an animal called Diekmann surrounded the town and forced everyone to come to the village market square. They told the people that they wanted to do an identity check. The soldiers went through the houses and forced everyone out, even those who were sick in bed. At about 3.30 p.m. they separated the women and children from the men. They forced the women and children to go into the church. Then from the entrance door they opened fire on them with machine guns and threw hand grenades at them. When they were all dead they covered the bodies with wood and chairs from the church and set fire to them. The men had been separated into three groups, taken to different parts of the town and machine-gunned down. In all 642 men women and children were killed. The youngest one was a seven-month old baby boy.

One woman managed to escape from the church by jumping out of a window at the back of the altar. Another woman and her baby who tried to do the same were both shot dead. After the massacre the Germans burned all the bodies and set fire to the town. A seven-year old boy who had stayed with his father managed to escape as the men were being marched off. He ran through a backyard garden and was shot at by a soldier. He dropped to the ground and played dead even when the soldier kicked him to see if he was really dead. Later he ran away and stumbled face to face onto another German soldier who, instead of shooting him, told him to run away as fast as he could.

The following day some German troops came back to 'tidy up' the place. They started to bury some of the dead but by lunchtime they gave up and went. We arrived mid morning on the Monday. With the Citroën car and the Bren gun sticking out of it and us four with our FFI arm bands it was quite obvious that we were *Maquisards*.

Some officials and various social groups were already there. Many local farmers and inhabitants from nearby villages were also there to assist. They had tried to identify the bodies but it was impossible. Most of them were burnt beyond recognition. In all I think only fifty odd bodies were officially identified. Although the officials and the social groups were public servants of the Vichy regime nothing was said to us at first. All we got were dirty looks. After an hour or so some of the helpers came over and abused us, saying that we were responsible for what had happened. Bob and Guy argued with them at length but the driver and I thought that in their resentment their argument had merit. So we kept out of it. We did not stay there long. We had a quick walk around the town, it was unbelievable to realise that human beings could do that sort of thing to other human beings in cold blood. By the time we left they had set out to bury them all without identification.

# 9

# THE CRASH

## JULY 1944

One night I was on parachute duty again with Bob and a dozen or so other men. It was in the early hours of 23 July 1944. We had been there for quite a while when we finally heard a plane coming. I think that Bob tried to contact it but we could not see it. We were wondering whether we should light the fires when suddenly out of nowhere a big four-engine plane, coming very low over the paddock, hit the ground and exploded a long way back from where we were. We all ran to where the plane had crashed. The wreckage was in flames. There was nothing we could do. There was a small farm a little further back. Bob and a couple of the boys went there to ask for help while we stayed at the crash site unable to do anything.

Later when Bob came back we sent a message to the chateau to tell all the men to come over. We walked closer to the wreck.

The fuselage was burning fiercely and from time to time we could hear small explosions. We could also hear cartridges blowing up in the fire. We just stood there unable to get close because of the flames. After a while the flames died down but there was still nothing we could do. By daylight only the fuselage was still burning. On the ground, not far from the body of the plane, we saw one of the crew lying down flat on his back. His parachute was unfolded and still attached to him. We decided to try to get to him in case he was still alive but when we got there he was dead. He was wearing a Royal Air Force uniform with a CANADA tag at the top of his sleeves. I think he was a lieutenant. Bits of wreckage of the plane were everywhere.

By then our entire company of the *Maquis* had arrived with a friend of mine called Lacouture. They took position around the place in case the Germans attracted by the fire decided to investigate. I knew Lacouture from Confolens before I joined the *Maquis*. He was now a lieutenant in our group. He immediately detailed me and a few others to help him 'clean up' as best we could. We found two more crew dead but intact and one that we could see still burning inside the fuselage. On the ground we came across body parts but it wasn't clear whether they belonged to only one man. From what we assessed at the time the plane had had a crew of five.

One of the two bodies which we thought were intact, had a tree laying across him. We could not figure out how that could have happened. It was as if the tree had been blown off on top of him after he was lying dead on the ground. He was fully dressed. We arranged to lift the tree and pull him out but as we did he came apart; bowels and intestines were strewn all over the grass. By then we had become accustomed to the gore and managed to perform quite well in spite of it. The body parts were collected in hessian bags to be consolidated later by more experienced people. Try as we did apparently we never found them all. These parts were all naked. I picked up a leg, an entire leg from the hip down which would have been inside a pair of trousers with a sock and a shoe or boot on, but it was naked. The blast must have blown all the clothing off the poor devil as it blew him apart.

The fuselage kept burning and we had no water to put the fire out. For three hundred yards (about 275 metres) around the main body of the plane the ground was strewn with plane debris, weapons, boxes of ammunition, some of them still intact and many containers, still attached to their parachutes. Some were in good condition others were damaged; some had been blown open and were empty. By midday the fire was almost out but the wreckage was still too hot to get the last crew's incinerated body out. It was done the next day.

Some farmers had arrived with bullocks and were dragging the debris close to the main body of the plane. We spent the day collecting weapons, ammunition and all other military supplies. That day I also got myself a handgun, a Smith & Wesson revolver and a uniform, an English battledress. We also collected all the containers and parachutes. The farmers told us that they would hide the debris of the plane with branches and trees when they were finished. The crash site was to be completely camouflaged. Lacouture went back to the chateau in mid afternoon, I stayed there until about 5pm then I went back with the last truck. Since I was now a sergeant I had to play the part and shoulder the responsibilities that went with it.

Two days later we all assembled at the Brillac cemetery for the funerals. Six coffins were on the back of two carts. Apparently the few body parts that we had picked up had actually belonged to two different individuals. That funeral was an elaborate affair. Several other groups of *Maquis* were there also. There must have been three or four hundred men there. There was a man wearing an English uniform taking photographs of the proceedings. Many of the villagers also attended.

Years later I learned that the six poor devils whom that night had tragically given up their lives to supply us from England with weapons and ammunitions were:

Flying Officer E. C. OKE, 22, Royal Canadian Air Force, Pilot.
Flight Sergeant T. M. GALVON, 21, Royal Canadian Air Force, Navigator.
Flight Sergeant L. A. HIGGINS, 27, Royal Canadian Air Force, Air Bomber.
Flight Sergeant R. G. CARROTHERS, 21, Royal Canadian Air Force, Air Gunner.
Flying Officer A. S. MIDDLETON, 25, Royal Air Force, Wireless Operator.
Flight Engineer R. A. WILKINS, 22, Royal Air Force, probably Co-pilot.

They were all members of the 620 Sqdn. Based at RAF Fairford west of London. Forty-five years later, during a holiday in France, I returned to Brillac with my wife. I wanted to pay my respects to these six brave men who that night had given their lives to supply us with what we needed to fight the Germans. It was a moving reminder of a period of my life which I wish had never happened.

A few days later my squad was sent to another *Maquis* which had lost a lot of men in a battle with the Germans. This *Maquis* was called Bir Akem. Even after all this time I didn't know that *Maquis* had names. In my asking I was told that our *Maquis* was called Foch, after the famous French First World War Marshall.

*Maquis Bir Akem* was situated quite a long way from *Maquis Foch*, on the other side of Confolens past the village of Ansac where my brother Phillip was living with the Merciers. We passed the village in the dark and I did not see my brother. We arrived at Bir Akem late at night and we were made very welcome by the men. They were all drunk. Whereas in the Maquis Foch we drank cider, in this one they drank wine, and plenty of it as we immediately found out. We also discovered that as a Maquis they were a lot more active than us at the Maquis Foch. There was something on almost every day.

Beside my little nest slept two fellows who had joined up together. They both originally came from Paris. One was called *le chat*, the cat, the other *la carotte* probably because his hair was bright red. Compared to the others there they were fully grown men. Before the war they had both been clowns at the Winter Circus in Paris and now, in the middle of our darkest hours, whether utterly drunk or quite sober they still managed to make us laugh. I became quite friendly with them. I enjoyed their company and their sense of humour, perhaps because we all came from a big city.

As I said there was something on every day or night. Not always spectacular performances or big battles but we were kept at it non-stop. Attacking a German truck. Blowing up a railway line. Blocking up a road by blowing trees down across it.

Painting the mile stones on the side of the roads with tar to obliterate the names of the towns and the distances between them. That made it difficult for the German convoys to find their way. That sort of thing kept us busy when there was nothing more important to do.

One night, however, we set out to attack La Braconne. It was a German ammunition depot and extremely well defended. Apparently we had been advised by the resistance that it contained dozens of trucks and jeeps and cannons and fuel drums and mountains of ammunition. The whole Maquis was involved, a miserable forty or so men. Full of guts but with very little else. The order had been to surround the place first, (forty or so men), then attack, go in and blow everything up. It was a joke. We never even got close enough to see the fence let alone to see what was inside.

Before we even managed to take up positions the Germans were already firing at us with machine guns. They could not really see us, they were firing at random, but we could not see them either. All we could see, at times, were the flames of their machine guns, and there were a lot of them. We were aiming at the flames hoping to hit the man who had his finger on the trigger, but it didn't seem to work. After about twenty minutes of fierce firing, getting nowhere, we were ordered to pull back. That turned out to be the worst part of the so-called attack.

A lot of the men anxious to leave simply stood up and ran away. Although it was pitch dark and the Germans could not see us, the random firing of the machine guns then became more effective. I could hear a lot of our men being hit. And to add insult to injury, because we had been told to surround the place, in the dark we had lost all sense of orientation. We had no idea where the trucks were to get back to them. Then the machine guns stopped firing and I could hear men running in the dark. I realised that the Germans were now coming after us. By pure chance I made contact with four other men. They were as lost as I was. We just ran for our lives, we didn't know where to, but we ran. Later we came across a dirt road and we didn't know which way to go, right or left. By the time we decided it was evident that we were not being chased anymore. Everything was silent. I forgot which direction we took but at day-break we deduced that we had taken the right one. Later that morning we were picked up along that road by a Citroën from the Maquis.

We had lost quite a number of men, but by then I did not want to know what our losses were anymore. All I knew was that at times we were being sacrificed for nothing. Courage itself has extreme value but it has none if it is simply being wasted. When we got back to the camp I saw three wounded men lying down in a corner. They were not being attended to. We had no medics anyway. One of them died the next day. I didn't know any of them. Le Chat and La Carrote were still around as jovial as ever.

# 10

# THE GERMANS ALSO HAD EARS

## AUGUST 1944

On 15 August the second front landing took place in Provence at Cavalaire, near St Tropez on the Mediterranean. It was a combined effort of English, American and French troops. Paratroopers had been dropped inland, near Le Muys, the night before. The entire operation had been a great success and within a few days Toulon and Marseilles were in the hands of the Allies. We foolishly assumed that now we had the Germans on the run. We were very soon to find out better.

The leaders of the Bir Akem Maquis one day decided to 'liberate' a town nearby. I am not quite sure whether my memory serves me correctly but I think the place was called Montenboeuf. The Bir Akem Maquis had a Citroën car with a loudspeaker fitted on the roof. It was used for public address and sometimes to play the *Marseillaise*. To add injury to stupidity, those who had planned the 'liberation' of Montenboeuf had decided to have the Citroën lead the convoy of Maquis trucks while loudly playing the *Marseillaise* on the loudspeaker. The idea was to let the people of the town know in advance that we were coming to liberate them. Whoever's idea this had been had obviously not realised that the Germans also had ears. As we came around a bend in the road, almost at the entrance of the town, the Germans were patiently waiting for us.

The Citroën was the first to cop it. It virtually disappeared. It must have got a direct hit from an anti-tank gun. The trucks were next. The Germans opened fire with machine guns. There were four or five of our trucks in line. I was in the second one. Some of the trucks stopped, others where the drivers had been hit just ran off the road. I threw my Bren down over the side and jumped off. I managed to crawl to a ditch at the side of the road, put my face into the dirt and with a mouth full of grass I waited. I must have been there at least a week; it certainly felt that long, before I was able to crawl back to a safer place.

By then the Germans were shooting at the trucks with anti-tank guns. Many were burning fiercely, some still had bodies inside the cabin and in the back. Somehow one of our men managed to get back to one of the trucks and got it going. He drove it backwards along the road whence we had come and disappeared out of sight. Some of us later were able to reach that truck. We waited there for a long time, always at the ready in case the Germans decided to come after us. A few more men came, but not many. Eventually we left and drove back to the camp. That liberation party had been another debacle. I lost my Bren gun assistant. I knew that one; his name was Gary. His father had been the railway station Master in Confolens.

That night we drank a lot of wine. It looked as if it was the end of the *Bir Akem Maquis*. Le Chat and La Carrote were no longer with us. We had lost most of the leaders too, they had been in the Citroën with the loudspeaker when it was hit.

The next day I rounded up what was left of my squad. We were only six or seven left. I explained that the *Bir Akim Maquis* was virtually finished and that we should return to the *Maquis Foch*. I didn't have to say it twice, they were all for it. I went around the camp and found an old Chenard & Walker; a sedan motorcar painted grey with a gazogene at the back. It was a wood burner; it used the gas from the slow combusting wood in the gazogene to run the engine. It had belonged to a doctor in Confolens and had been requisitioned by the *Maquis*. After a couple of hours of desperate attempts, we finally got it going. We all cramped in and drove back to the chateau.

When we arrived we were welcomed by the boys, but Bob and Lacouture wanted to know why we had come back. As I explained to them what had happened Bob relented slightly but I could sense that he was not comfortable with my decision. He wanted to know if the boys had talked me into deciding to come back. When I told him that it was initially my decision he wanted to know if I had had enough. That wasn't it at all but I did point out that I, and most of us, had had enough of these senseless acts of bravado, which served no purpose and attracted no recompense.

Human lives were at stake and the fact that we were at war

did not minimise their value. If any were to be spent it would have to be in quest of a tangible benefit not some foolish act of immolation which gave no reward.

One thing led to another and suddenly I found myself, unloading at the top of my voice, what had been on my mind now for many months. The balance between the value to the Allied Forces of our activities against the Germans, against the atrocious reprisals by the Germans on the civilian population for what we did. My argument was not to stop all operations but not to simply keep active in order to occupy ourselves in pointless engagements. Engagements which cost *Maquis* and civilian lives and which had absolutely no influence whatsoever on the ultimate outcome of the war in Europe.

'It's war, it's war' that's all he would say but I could sense that in a very small measure I had got across to him. He was a full grown man and I was still only a bit of a kid.

For a few days he left me alone. He didn't speak to me. On my side I felt that I had to do something. I knew that Confolens had been liberated by one of the *Maquis* and that a Resistance Headquarter had been established there. Since that vociferous discussion with Bob we had not had any actions against the Germans. There seemed to be none around. I think they were either in the North fighting the Allies who had landed in Normandy or in the South fighting those who had landed at Cavalaire.

One day I went to see Bob. I unloaded on him an idea, which I had been nursing in my mind for about a week. I pointed out that the Germans were now obviously on the run. That those fighting against the Allies in the South of France would escape to Germany through the Rhone valley and that the activities of the *Maquis* in central France were virtually over. He kind of agreed with me and asked me what that discussion was really all about. I told him that the war in Europe, even though not over, was already decided. I also told him that the war in the Pacific was still going full strength; that the Japanese were still occupying the Dutch East Indies. And that since I was Dutch, for me the war would go on for a long time yet.

I told him that I wanted to join the Dutch force, which had landed in the South of France. There was nothing he could say and he didn't say anything. He asked me how did I intend to get across the German lines to get to the Allies in the South. I told him that I would decide that when I had to face it. He told me to report to the Resistance Headquarters in Confolens and that the decision was theirs. The next day he got someone to drive me to Confolens. We parted on good terms. After the war I was decorated with La Croix du Combatant, which is the highest French honour bestowed on a member of the *Maquis*.

# 11

# OFF TO ALGIERS

## SEPTEMBER 1944

At the Resistance Headquarter in Confolens I repeated what I had told Bob to someone who appeared to be in charge. His name, if I remember well, was Mr Guillemot. He was a *geule cassée* from the First World War. He had no face. His face had been blown apart and was now completely disfigured. He wore a black cloth mask over his face down to his upper lip and tied to his ears. He turned out to be a very nice and sincere gentleman. He appeared to be very interested in what I had in mind and went out of his way to help. I was issued with an *Ordre de Mission* which was a direct order for me to make my way to the Allied forces in the South of France to join the Dutch Army.

Since the nature of the Order contemplated my passing from the German front lines to the Allies' front line, the Order was folded and nailed inside the heel of a civilian pair of shoes. I was also given some money and a bicycle to make the trip. The very nice gentleman probably thought that I had lost all my marbles and that I was anxious to commit suicide. But being one of the heads of the Resistance Headquarter he could not possibly dissuade me to undertake such a patriotic adventure.

The next morning I was on my way. It was early September. I had decided to play it bold. The bolder the better. I took no luggage. No food or sandwiches, not even drinking water. I wore a short sleeved shirt, shorts, ankle high socks and of course the shoes, very loosely laced in case I had to discard them in a hurry. My idea was to try to look like any of the local kids not going anywhere, simply riding his bicycle. Sometime during the day or at night I would try to buy something to eat and have a drink of water. Never in a village but from farms that I was passing by along the way. Often when I told the farmers where I was heading to, they would give me the food for nothing. I was often given eggs which I would suck raw through two little holes. I detested that but it was a means to an end. It kept me fit.

On the third day of my trip, at about eleven in the morning, I came to a long column of about twenty-five or thirty German trucks. They were parked on the side of the road facing south, the same direction that I was going. They were full of soldiers. Probably on their way to reinforce the German army fighting the Allied forces which had landed in Provence. By the time I saw them they would also have seen me, so instead of turning back I just biked right past them; just one of the local kids riding his bike. It worked and it did work again on several other occasions after that.

Before I left Confolens I had memorised the names of the various villages and towns that I had to go through to reach Marseilles. As I mentioned earlier, in those days in France, the names of the villages and towns were painted on the milestones with the distances to and from. I had forgotten that one of the activities of the *Maquis* had been to obliterate that kind of information with black paint to confuse the Germans. So in various places where this had been done it did confuse me also. I got lost a few times.

On the fourth day I came across discarded German trucks, in the middle of the road. Later I saw some that had been burned out. Later still I came across damaged cannons and destroyed tanks and other dumped war materials. Further on, the destroyed guns and tanks and jeeps were no longer German. They were destroyed and abandoned American materials with the white star painted on them. I knew then that I was in the American sector. I had obviously crossed the lines without seeing either a German or an American soldier dead or alive.

About mid afternoon I came into a village and it was full of American soldiers and trucks and tanks and what have you. I rode to a black sergeant who appeared to be directing traffic and I asked him where I was. He seemed suspicious at first; the fact that I spoke English and didn't know where I was. But when I told him who I was and where I had come from he couldn't be helpful enough. He took me into what had been a bar and asked me if I was hungry and told me to wait. This bar had been turned into a kind of commanding post. There were other soldiers there; some minor ranked officers all very busy. When the sergeant came back he had a map. He also had a tin of baked beans and a small bar of fruit paste. I then decided that beans were definitely the fighting man's staff food. He showed me on the map where I was and pointed to the city of Avignon very close by.

'If you wait for a while I'll probably find someone to give you a lift there', he said, but since Avignon was only a few kilometres further I decided to cycle there by myself.

When I got there I went straight to the railway station where I was told that the line to Marseilles was damaged in several places and no one could say when it would be open again. Someone told me where the FFI Headquarters were and there I went. There was a man there who appeared to be in charge. I told him that I had an Order de Mission in the heel of my shoe and that I had to go to Marseilles to join the Dutch Army. He said, 'Where is that shoe?' So I took it off my foot and gave it to him.

I said, 'Get a chisel and a hammer and I'll show it to you.' He took the shoe, walked away with it, and was gone for quite a while. When he came back he was reading the Order de Mission and had my shoe in his other hand fully repaired with the heel back on. He said that he didn't know whether the Dutch Army had Headquarters in Marseilles but that he was trying to arrange transportation to take a few people, who like me, had to report to Marseilles urgently. By then it was dark and I was hungry again. The baked beans and the fruit paste had gone a long way. This time I wasn't so lucky. I still had a few francs in my pocket but there was no food to be had anywhere so I went back to the Headquarters, sat in the hall there and decided to sit out the night.

At about 4am a man came in and asked me if I was the one who had to go to Marseilles. I said yes and went with him. We

These are photographs of the Canadian airmen's funeral at Brillac, taken
at the time by a man in English uniform. I saw him taking the photos
and recently asked the Lord Mayor of Brillac if these photos were
available. He was kind enough to send me a copy of them and an
authorisation to use them in this book.

After the massacre, Oradour-sur-Glane was left intact and made into a mausoleum open to the public. The town was rebuilt on an adjacent site.

The pass used as a Maquis to travel.

This photo was taken in England, 1944.

In the army camp at Hollandia in Northern New Guinea in 1945. The two fellows on the left were being sent to Biak Island. I am on the right.

Japanese printed half-guilder used by the population of Indonesia during the Japanese occupation.

At the army camp at Hollandia in Northern New Guinea in
1945. That's me on the left.

In Australia, 1945.

After the war, I became an animal catcher. This is a photo taken when I was catching animals near Mount Duval, north of Armidale in Australia.

Crates of kangaroos ready for export.
We are waiting for the trucks to arrive.

Anzac Day march in Brisbane 2005. That's me on the right.

walked around for a while and ended up in a courtyard. There was an old bus there fitted with a wood burning gazogene at the back and about a dozen other people waiting. One of them was a woman. Somehow the driver had been told that I was an FFI sergeant. He gave me a Michelin map of the area and asked me to sit beside him and guide him through smaller departmental roads to Marseilles because the main roads were all blocked with military junk.

So we got on our way. It was difficult to navigate. All road signs had been taken off and the milestones had been painted over. We ended up in a few cul-de-sacs and by midday we were barely halfway there. We stopped to refuel the gazogene and stretch our legs. During that break I spoke to the woman passenger. She was going to see her husband in a hospital in Marseilles. He had been wounded during the landing in Provence. He had been with the Free French under De Gaulle since 1940 and she hadn't seen him since. That break was not a lunch break it was only to restock the gazogene with firewood. I was starving and I suppose we all were but it wasn't nice to show it so no one said anything.

At about 3pm we finally joined the main road to Marseilles at Salon. The road itself was clear. Wrecked trucks and jeeps and blown-up tanks had been bulldozed off the centre of the road and were piled up in the ditches along each side of it. By then we knew we only had forty or so kilometres to go. The going was good and by 5.30pm we were pulling up in front of the Saint Charles railway station in Marseilles. The driver told me that he was going to the Fort Saint Nicholas with the bus and asked me if he could drop me somewhere. I got off at the

*Canebiere* and went home. I didn't know whether my parents were still there. When I knocked on the door no one answered. Our next floor up neighbour heard me and came out on her landing. She told me that my father was still there but that my mother had been sent away somewhere in central France to hide.

I went upstairs and stayed with them until a little after 7pm when I heard my father coming. I went down and we had a big hug. We hadn't seen each other for over two years. Not since that night at the railway station when I and my brothers had been sent away. He was thrilled to see me and I was thrilled to see him. He had received news of my brothers, Phillip and Edward, and told me that he had sent my mother to Limoges for her safety. He thought that by now she would be somewhere near Confolens on her way to see my brothers. He said he knew that I had been in the *Maquis* and that he had been terribly worried about it.

He laughed when I told him that I was made a sergeant only because I could speak English. He thought that by now I would leave the war alone. He was somewhat disturbed when I told him that I was only being transferred to the Dutch army. He told me that as far as he knew there was no Dutch contingent in the forces which had landed at Cavalaire. I told him that in any case I had to report to the FFI Headquarter in Marseilles. I explained to him that the *Ordre de Mission* which I had in my pocket more or less gave me no choice but to proceed with it and join the Dutch Army wherever it was.

That night we sat down to a remarkably good meal. He brought out a bottle of red wine. It wasn't a particularly good bottle of wine but it was still wartime and it was wine. That night he treated me like a man and we both finished the bottle. When I asked him where the fancy food came from he told me that the Captain of a Dutch Navy ship in the harbour had sent it to him only a couple of days before. We talked until the early hours of the morning. He brought out the bottom third of a bottle of Brandy and we cleaned it up, talking about the Germans, Hitler, De Gaulle, Churchill, the Jews and the Americans.

The next morning I reported to the FFI Headquarters in Marseilles. It was combined with the Free French contingent and now I was talking to real army Officers. I showed them my *Ordre de Mission*. One of them told me that he would look into it. He asked me if I had a place to stay. When I said I had he told me to come back the next day.

When I fronted up again the following morning I asked to see the same Officer, I can't remember his name. He came over and told me he was taking care of it and asked me to wait. And wait I did. Hours of it. When he finally showed up again he told me that there was no Dutch Army in Southern France but that there was a contingent In North Africa. He handed me another *Ordre de Mission* to report to the Free French Headquarters in Nice and a rail pass to get there. I spent the rest of the day in Marseilles and the next morning I said good bye to my father, walked all the way to Saint Charles Railway station and boarded a train to Nice.

I arrived there in early afternoon and reported immediately to the Free French Headquarters. The officer I was to see wasn't there and I was told to wait. He didn't show up that day. That night I took a room in a small hotel in a street nearby. The next morning, when I arrived at the Headquarters the man was there. He had my *Ordre de Mission* in his hand. He kept calling me sergeant even though I was dressed in civilian clothes. It was the first time that I had been addressed by my rank and it pleased me very much. Mind you it was going to be the last time for quite a while. He gave me a letter addressed to the Dutch Consul in Algiers which I wasn't allowed to read and told me to front up at the Headquarters at 6am, not the following morning but the day after that. I rang my father and he suggested that I'd go back to Marseilles and return to Nice the following day. That would give us another night together.

I got on the train and went to Marseilles. My father met me at the station and we walked together down Boulevard Dugomier to the Dutch Consulate. There he also wrote a letter to the Dutch Consul in Algiers. This one I was allowed to read. It introduced me to his colleague as his son, asking him to do everything he could to assist me in what he described to him as 'This stupid fixation to carry on the war' or words to that effect. When I tried to start an argument on the subject he simply said 'You don't have to give it to him if you don't want to.'

He had work to do so I went home. That night we ate the rest of the Captain's gift and drank another bottle of wine, which came out of nowhere. The next morning when I woke up my father had already gone. I had a cup of powdered coffee which was completely new to me. Obviously invented in America and imported by the American soldiers. I left and started to walk to Saint Charles Station. On the way I stopped at the Consulate and said good bye to my father and off I went to Nice.

On arrival I took a room in the same hotel where I had stayed a couple of nights before not far from the Headquarters. I lay on the bed and spent the rest of the day thinking about what was going to happen tomorrow. I knew I was to go to Algiers but I did not know how.

By 5am I was already seated in the corridor of the Free French Headquarters waiting to be picked up. The sergeant behind the desk brought me a cup of coffee and had one himself but we did not talk. A little before six a jeep pulled up outside, the driver came in and asked me if I was the chap that he was supposed to pick up at six. I said 'yes' and probably since I was the only one there other than the desk sergeant, he believed me. I went out with him. There was another sergeant sitting in the front of the jeep, I hopped in the back, we said hullo and we were on our way. We drove to the airport. It wasn't very far.

When we arrived there the driver and the other sergeant went to one of the offices. I was told to wait in the jeep. A few minutes later the driver came back and drove me to a large twin engine bomber standing on the tarmac beside a few other planes. There were a number of officers standing there talking to each other. I got off the jeep and stood there also. I felt awful. The others were all French Army and Air force officers. I was only a sergeant and it didn't even show because I was still in civilian clothes.

There I was just a kid amongst senior French military brass. I had never been so embarrassed in my life before, so I sort of stood apart from the others. Very soon one of the Air Force officers came over to me and asked me if I was the one who had

101

to go to Algiers. I said yes, and he told me that he was the pilot and that the plane was going to Tunis. He said that other arrangements would be made in Tunis to take me to Algiers. He never asked me the reason for my trip and I didn't tell him.

The plane was obviously not meant for passengers. I was the last to get in and most of the officers were already sitting on the floor. I went to the back of the fuselage and did the same. We took off, turned over the city and headed south over the sea. I saw the city not through a window because there were none but through an unoccupied machine gun turret on the top aft of the plane as it banked to make its turn. I was terribly excited, it was the first time ever that I had been in a plane. In less than an hour we were coming down again. I didn't know where we were. We landed and taxied to a small hangar. We all got out to stretch our legs; sitting on the floor was taking its toll. Inside the hangar, a Royal Air Force sergeant was dishing out ham sandwiches and orange drinks. That's when I discovered that we were in Ajaccio, in Corsica.

About two and a half hours later we were coming down again, this time in Tunis. All the officers were picked up by different jeeps and staff cars. The sergeant behind the desk told me that I would be flying to Algiers very first thing next morning and that I could bunk there for the night. I wanted to go into town but the airport was a long way away from the city and there was no facility to commute. So I settled for the local resort, I was given a plate full of ham sandwiches and spent the night in a barrack full of beds. I was the only guest there.

That 'very first thing in the morning' turned out to be soon after lunch when I boarded an American DC3. This plane did have windows but in the middle of each plastic pane in the windows was a hole big enough to poke the muzzle of a rifle through and shoot if the opportunity arose. It had seats too. Two long metal seats extending the length of the plane each side of the fuselage. There were about twenty of us in there. All in uniform except me. An American soldier sitting next to me attempted to speak to me in French. He was delighted when I put him out of his misery and answered him in English.

We arrived in Algiers late in the afternoon. It was mid September 1944. The sergeant at the desk at the airport knew that I had to report to the Dutch Consulate. He told me that he would ring them first to see if it was still open. It wasn't, so I told him that I would go there first thing in the morning. I was offered accommodation for the night but decided to seek my own in the city.

An army bus waiting there took me and some other servicemen to Square Bresson, and there I was, in Algiers. I took a small room in a hotel in one of the alleyways cutting across towards the top of the city. It was cheap and nasty, but clean enough.

That night I stumbled into a bar full of French soldiers. In conversation they wanted to know what it had been like in France during the German occupation. I told them as much as I knew. The life in the *Maquis* that I knew did not exactly reflect the standards of ordinary French civilian life under the German Occupation. What they wanted to know was how the French people had fared during the occupation and there I couldn't help them much. We drank a lot of Muscatel, a sweet popular local wine, and by midnight I was in bed.

103

# 12

# IN THE ARMY

## SEPTEMBER 1944

The next morning I enquired where the Dutch Consulate was and I went there. I met the Consul and gave him the sealed letter that the Officer in Nice had ordered me to give him and also the one my father had written. He told me that the Dutch Contingent in Algiers had not landed with the Americans. He said that it was made up of Dutch ex-French Foreign Legionnaires who had deserted the French Foreign Legion when the Vichy Government had ordered them to fight the Americans at the time of the landing in Morocco. He told me that there were only a couple of hundred men there and that they were due to be transferred to England very soon. He made a phone call for someone to pick me up and in the mean time we talked. We talked about my father, France, the Jews, the *Maquis* and finally me.

About an hour later a huge man in uniform was shown into the Consul's office and stood at attention. He was a sergeant. The Consul introduced me as a new recruit; I said good bye and left with the sergeant. I later learned that his name was Kranzden. The camp was hundreds of square tents rigged up in the centre of a racecourse. It was a British Army camp. Sergeant Kranzden took me to one of the tents and pointed to a canvas stretcher.

'That's yours, Nyst,' he said. 'Now come with me.'

He took me to one of the barracks. The store was run by a British Sergeant. There I was outfitted with a complete English battledress uniform. Just like the one that I had appropriated at the crash of the plane near Brillac. This time the outfit was more complete. I was given a white kit bag, shirts and socks and shoes and a cap and underwear and even two rectangular mess gears and a canteen. The British sergeant in charge of the stores also gave me two little curved tags with the word 'Netherlands' embroidered on them. These, he said, were to be sewn at the top of the sleeves near the shoulders. When I went back to the tent another soldier was there. He was old enough to be my father. I introduced myself to him and he told me that his name was Koertz.

The tent was comfortable. It was the normal American square type tent with a high centre pole and a shorter one on each corner. There were four canvas stretchers in it. The floor was dirt but grass free and a few wooden crates were there for storage. I immediately changed into my uniform and felt a lot better for it. Now of course I was just an ordinary soldier again. In the afternoon the third occupant of the tent came in. His name was

Max Beer. He and Koertz were both ex-Legionnaires. The fourth stretcher remained empty until we left. With a piece of plywood on it we used it as a table Although we were in the army and on active duty we were not drilling or exercising. We had the whole day to ourselves, obviously we were waiting for something. Over the next few days I gradually met some of the other Dutch soldiers. Some of them would come to our tent to talk and drink. Sometimes we went to their tent.

Before the war my father had sent me to an old retired Dutch school teacher living in Marseilles who had taught me to speak Dutch. I thought that I could speak Dutch but I was wrong. Listening to these old blokes I could hardly understand what they were talking about, although they seemed to understand me when I spoke in Dutch to them. I later learned that their Dutch was so full of swear words and expletives that unless one had lived with it one could not possibly understand a single word. Of course Mr Grant, my Dutch teacher in Marseilles, had overlooked the necessity to encumber my vocabulary with the necessary extras contained in the most swear loaded and swear assisted language in the world. Fortunately it didn't take me long to catch up. I had good teachers and as in my first few days at school I soon mastered the new version.

At six in the evening there was always a bus or a truck going into Algiers. I went a few times but it was embarrassing. The first stop would invariably be a brothel. I did not want to partake but it was either standing alone in the back of the truck or going inside and wait for my mates. This I did a few times. I would go inside and wait with them while they patiently waited their turn. Those who had already been accommodated would then

106

come and join me and wait for the others. At that time I had never been with a woman and I was certainly not going to break the ice with these old tarts who were assuring me a good time at the cost of God only knew what beside the money. Especially after what I had been told about venereal diseases. After this unfortunate compulsory initial stop we would all go into town to have a good time drinking or fighting. One night I missed the truck going back to the camp. I had met some young Dutchmen in a bar who had arrived that day in Algiers. They had escaped from Europe through Spain and Morocco and now wanted to join the Dutch Army but did not know where or how. Noticing the 'Netherland' tag at the top of the sleeve of my uniform they wanted to know more about it. I told them to go and see the Consul. We talked and drank a lot of Muscatel. One thing led to another and before I knew it I realised that the truck going back to the camp would have gone. I wished good luck to my new friends and decided to get myself a bed for the night. I was walking up one of the many short-cut alleys going uphill looking for a cheap hotel to stay the night when suddenly.... nothing. The next morning I woke up in a nice bed with clean white sheets, a hell of a sore neck and a beautiful nurse smiling at me. In English she asked me

'How do you feel soldier?'

It was a question I didn't know how to answer. Except for my neck I was feeling all right until I tried to sit up. Then I thought I was going to fall apart. The ward was not full. The nurse told me that I was in hospital, an American hospital. She said that I had been brought there the night before by two military police who had found me lying unconscious in an alley. Apparently assisted by them I sort of walked in. I certainly did not have any recollection of that. She also told me that I was naked and only because of the dog tag around my neck did they know that I was a soldier. They knew that I was not an American but they didn't know what else I was. Apparently I had been hit and stripped of my uniform and underwear and left in the alley.

After a while I made an extra effort to stand up and somehow managed it. I was wearing one of those white nightshirts open in the back. I told the nurse that I wanted to go immediately. She called a doctor who could not give a damn whether I stayed or left, so I told him that I would leave. Of course there was one problem. I had nothing to wear. I told the doctor where my camp was and he said he would call them. In the afternoon a Dutch sergeant brought me a pair of khaki shorts and a khaki shirt and took me back to camp in a jeep. Of course once there I was the laugh of the week.

A couple of days later, before breakfast, Sergeant Kranzden came into our tent and told us to pack and be ready to go sometime that morning. Straight after lunch we were taken by truck to the wharves where hundreds of soldiers were already getting aboard a ship.

After standing there for an hour or two our turn came and we climbed the gangway onto the *Eastern Prince*. It was an ex-cargo ship transformed into a troop transport. In places around the edge of the deck wooden latrines had been built overhanging the sea. They were elaborate affairs with accommodation for about a dozen men at a time seated side by side. If you fell through the hole you'd better have been wearing your lifejacket.

We were taken several decks down below and given a reasonable bunk. I had a bottom one and Max Beer had the bunk on top of me. We were down in the bowels of the ship with no portholes. It was the first time that I had ever been on a ship. I found it exciting and told Max. He warned me that it might be different once we put out to sea. At about 6pm dinner was brought down to our deck. We queued up for it and received a very good meal and a mess gear of tea. We had to eat off our knees sitting on my bunk. As we were having dinner we felt the boat move but after a few minutes we heard the anchor chain going overboard and we stopped again.

We went on deck after dinner. We were anchored there, close to land, with other ships nearby waiting for the convoy to be assembled. After it got dark most of the boys went down to their bunks but I stayed there. I was so excited I could not have slept anyway. I just stood there by the railing looking at the water. It was pitch black. No lights at all showing anywhere. After a while I sat down against a bulkhead and eventually fell asleep. Sometime later I was woken by one of the crew kicking my legs. He told me to go down below and I went to my bunk. When I woke up again I could feel that we were on our way. I didn't bother to wait for breakfast; I picked up my lifejacket and went straight up on deck. It was beautiful. The weather was fine, the sea was calm and all around us were ships of all kinds including several small war ships. I was really impressed to see such might. We weren't going very fast and I imagine that this was what a pre-war Mediterranean cruise would have been like. I decided to walk around to acquaint myself with the ship. On deck were all kinds of uniforms. Naval, Airforce and Army, all

English except for us Dutch. At about 10am the ship's siren started to blast. It was Emergency Station. We all went to a pre-determined location, put our lifejackets on and waited in ranks for the inspection. Later that morning, walking around the deck, I came across some of the Dutch boys that I had met in Algiers the night that I was bashed in the alley. They were in different uniforms than us; khaki shorts and safari jackets. We talked about all sorts of things until lunchtime when I went down below to eat.

That afternoon I lay in my bunk. I didn't sleep but thought about the 'emergency station' of that morning. I tried to work out how long it would take us to reach that station, scrambling up the different gangways with hundreds of other soldiers also wanting to get there as fast as they could. Somehow I didn't like the figure that I came up with. I didn't tell anyone, I kept it to myself. Max came in and told me that we could see Gibraltar. I went with him on deck and admired the scene. We weren't actually close but with a bit of concentration and a lot of imagination one could make out The Rock on the horizon on the starboard side. We stayed there until it started to get dark and went down below for dinner. When I got down I noticed empty forty-four gallon drums, with their lids off had been positioned between the bunks. I had no idea what they were there for, but it was in preparation of things to come.

An hour or so later, when we were in the Atlantic, I noticed that the loud conversation around our deck had singularly quietened down. Some men even appeared to have decided on an early night. Before much longer, a few men decided to pay an urgent visit to the forty-four gallon drums; inaugurating the set up by contributing the meal that they had eaten only an hour or so before. Now I knew what the drums were there for. It made me sick. I didn't vomit but I went straight up on deck and decided that I wasn't going down again. That night I discovered a spot on the deck, beside some coiled ropes on the seaboard side of a life boat. I spent the night there. I could not be seen from the deck and it became my spot. The sea was getting very rough and it was getting cooler but I slept very well. When I woke up we were heading north, the sea had become a lot worse. The green faced soldiers and airmen, leaning over the rails tossing their insides overboard were now a common sight. At times even some navy men joined in. I was keeping my fingers crossed and it seemed to help. I didn't know before that, that there was a connection between the fingers and the stomach but it worked. I didn't waste any of my meals. That night I stayed by the railings until only a few soldiers remained on deck, then without attracting attention I squeezed into my spot. I was cold but I felt I had a chance if things turned bad; I wasn't scared I was only being careful. Before long things did turn bad. Not for us, but for a ship astern of us to starboard. That was the right side of the ship where my spot was. I could see it all lying down on deck. The explosion wasn't very loud but it was spectacular to look at. It must have been a tanker. Huge big flames lit up the sky. Against it I could see the profile of a corvette zigzagging between the ships nearby but I did not see it do anything. Our ship did not summon 'Emergency stations' and we didn't stop or slow down. Within fifteen minutes or so the large flames died out and only small flames here and there seemed to persist. A lot of men came on deck to look and even though they were told to go below very few of them did. That order of course did not apply to me, I couldn't be seen. I stayed shivering with cold in my spot for the rest of the night. I did not sleep. The next day we were told that a tanker indeed had been torpedoed and that we might receive some of the injured crew. It was something to talk about and we did certainly talk about it.

We were told that U boats now concentrated more on the North Atlantic-America run and were not much of a threat any more in the Bay of Biscay. It was suggested that the loss of that tanker was probably only a one off attack. Nevertheless that day, when I went below for my lunch, I put on, underneath my battle dress, every single item of clothing that I had in my kit-bag. I spent the rest of the day on deck and that night I was prepared for the cold.

That very same night I also noticed that the latrines were fully occupied with standing room only for those who were waiting and no one ever came out. I realised that a lot of other men had done the same mental exercise as I had regarding the time it takes to reach the emergency station and had wisely acted accordingly. Towards midnight we were attacked again.

When I say we, I do not mean our ship, I mean the convoy. I heard an explosion in the distance and about twenty minutes later another one followed by a number of quick ones. I could not see anything but I wasn't going to lose my spot to see what was going on. The next morning the word got around that we had lost two more ships to U boats. Apparently no one else from our ship had seen anything to that effect during the night. They had heard the explosions but no one had seen anything. That morning I didn't bother about breakfast but when I went down to queue up for my lunch the atmosphere down there was unbelievable.

A horrible stench of vomit prevailed everywhere. All the forty-four gallon drums were three quarters full of it. Max was just about dead of sea sickness in his bunk and when I asked him if I could get him some food he answered me by retching like a dog. I knew exactly what he meant. I left the poor devil alone and was very relieved when I managed to get back on deck without being sick. I had my lunch on deck.

The next few days and nights went on without any spectacular events. The sea was still rough but more and more men now seemed to cope with it. At night we heard explosions but there was nothing to see. We were told that they were anti-submarine depth charges fired by the corvettes but we didn't really know for sure and didn't care. After a couple of weeks of this eventful sea voyage, one morning when I woke up the sea was a lot calmer. We still could not see land but the word got around that we were in the Irish Sea and probably going either to Liverpool or to Glasgow. We had not lost any more ships and with the end of the trip in sight the holiday cruise mood returned. We entered the Clyde in the afternoon and as we were proceeding into it somewhere on the starboard side was moored the *Queen Mary*. Of course it was a sight to see and no one wanted to miss it. Such was the attraction that the *Eastern Prince* suddenly developed a nasty list to starboard.

Nasty enough for the command to blast a 'battle station' signal on the ship's siren right there in the middle of the river in Glasgow. That took care of the list.

# 13

# IN ENGLAND AT WAR

## OCTOBER 1944

We eventually berthed. It was mid October 1944. On the wharf a band was playing. We were all told over the loudspeaker to go back to our station and wait there. We, the Dutch, did not have to wait long. We were asked to go on deck to disembark. As we came off the ship we were immediately loaded onto trucks. We were under guard. Seated at the back of each truck were two armed guards making sure that no one escaped. The trucks took us to the railway station. When we boarded the train the guards stayed with us. Through the night in conversing with them we were told that this was standard procedure and that everyone entering Britain had to be screened by security. The next morning we reached London.

We were taken by truck again, still under guard, to a special army camp at Cannon Park. There we each went through Customs and a lengthy interrogation. After that we were taken to a nice warm barracks and billeted there.

That camp contained all sorts of foreign forces men. There were French soldiers there, Poles, Dutch, Danes, Norwegian and many others. The food was excellent, we could read and play games but we could not get out. Not until we were cleared. One afternoon we heard a huge explosion not far outside the camp and that night we were told that it had been a doodle bug. One of Hitler's new secret weapons. It had done some damage but there were no casualties.

After four or five days I and some of the others who had come with me from Africa, were cleared and we were sent by truck to a Dutch Forces Sorting Centre at Earls Court. There the Dutch army had commandeered a whole street. Merloes Road. We were billeted in houses on both sides of the street. At 7am the roll-call and sick parade would take place outside in the street. After that we were free to do whatever we wanted unless we were summoned for special duty. During the day I often went to the movies. One night with a friend of mine, an ex-French Foreign Legionnaire from Algiers called Willy Hogerslag, and I went out to the West End. There were a lot of people in the streets.

We could hear them but we could not see them, we could not see anything. The blackout was very strict and for good reason. We were walking, clinging to the walls when we suddenly heard music coming out of a doorway. We entered, it was a dance hall. I seem to recall that it was called the Cafe de

Paris. It was in Leicester Square. We walked in to get warm. It was a lovely place full of atmosphere and pleasant music. It was crowded. Around the dance floor were tables and chairs with people drinking and talking. All around, upstairs from the dance floor was a balcony also with tables and chairs. We managed to get a table there and ordered some drinks.

I couldn't dance, or should I say that I had never danced before. Willy went downstairs to dance and I was left at the table by myself. Within a few minutes two RAF WAFS came up and asked if they could share our table. I said yes and we started to talk. I was asked why I was not dancing and I told them. They said it was easy and before long, one of them was hanging on to me on the dance floor downstairs. Actually it's not true, I was the one hanging on to her like grim death. It certainly was a new experience and I enjoyed every bit of it. I had never trodden on so many toes before in my life nor since, but before the night ended I could manage to go around the floor without having to say 'Sorry' more than five or six times. Having gained some confidence in this new exercise, I did find dancing a very pleasurable pastime.

With some of my friends we adopted a fairly regular routine to patronise the various London dance halls. The Hammersmith Palais and the Stage Door Canteen were our favourites. The Stage Door Canteen was in Piccadilly, not far from Piccadilly Circus on the left hand side going out towards Green Park. It was for Military personnel only. There were a lot of Americans there, males and females. It was on every night and was always crowded. We always had a lot of fun there. That's where I learned to jitterbug.

One Sunday afternoon I had been invited for tea by a girl that I had met at the Stage Door Canteen. She was an ATS and her parents lived in London. I arrived at about 3pm. Her father took me upstairs and proudly showed me his rifle. He was in the Home Guard. He had been in the First World War and we talked about the army for the rest of the afternoon. As darkness fell, I and the girl were sitting in the lounge on a settee in front of a large bay window. The girl's mother came in and told us that it was getting dark and that we ought to draw the heavy curtain across the window for the curfew. We did just that. As we sat down again a huge explosion occurred. We ended up flat on the floor and the curtain and all the glass in the window ended on top of us. It had been a V2, another one of Hitler's secret weapons. I wasn't hurt, the girl had a few glass cuts but she was all right. The lounge however was a mess and so were the upstairs rooms. The bomb had fallen on the other side of the park across the street, nearly a quarter of a mile away. Before long helpers came to assist and I went back to Merloes Road. I never saw that girl again.

One morning, after roll-call, I was told to report to the office. When I got there, about a dozen other soldiers were already waiting. All of us there had come from Africa. We were told that we were being assigned. We were instructed to attend at a doctor's surgery somewhere at the back of Regent Street for our medical. After a bit of searching we eventually found the place. It was a building full of doctors' surgeries but where we had to report was a Dutch Military Medical Centre. It occupied the entire floor. The usual took place. We were made to strip and each in turn was attended by the Medical Officer.

When my turn came the Officer took both my hands and said, 'Your right forearm seems to be a little thinner than the left, have you had an accident?.

I told him, 'No, I had polio when I was five.'

He then asked me if this was the only trace of it left and I told him, 'Yes'.

'You'll be all right then,' he said.

Next we queued up in front of the assigning officer who automatically shovelled the whole bunch of us into the KNIL The Netherlands East Indies Army. Why? Because we all came from Africa. We were, according to him, colonials and accustomed to a tropical climate. Little did he know that my only tropical acquaintance had only been two months in Algiers. My friend Willy, who was old enough to be my father and had spent ten years in the French Foreign Legion, was looking forward to be going back home to Holland. He asked if he could be assigned to the Princess Irene Brigade, which was then fighting in northern France. Whatever reply he got he ended up in Australia with the rest of us. Max Beer was the only one of us who got away with it and I never saw him again.

The following day we were taken by truck to a railway station and then by train to Wolverhampton. There were over a hundred of us on that train and as usual we had no idea where we were going. We knew that we were going north, nothing else. It was only when we were told to get off the train that we discovered our destination.

The Dutch Army camp in Wolverhampton was immense. We were taken to three barracks, miles away from the general amenities and told to pick a bed. That we did. Each of these barracks contained about thirty beds. There was a wood stove somewhere in the centre and a pillow and blankets on each bed. A kind of narrow bookshelf was there beside the bed for our clothes. We soon settled down as best we could. We were all shivering. Even with the stove going on full blast it was extremely cold inside. When it got dark we heard over the loud speaker that it was dinner time. We were all starving but we didn't know where to go. That was another amusing experience which thankfully ended well. When we finally found the mess, it was nice and warm and the food was superb. That night it was 'stampot'. You have to be Dutch to know what that is: potatoes and cabbage with pork sausages. When you're cold and hungry there's nothing like it to bring you back to life. While we stayed there we had stampot about four times a week.

We went to the store the next day to be outfitted. Thankfully, we were allowed to keep our woolen battledress and topcoat but we were issued with shorts and safari jackets and a huge colonial helmet with the brim pointed at the front and square at the back. It was made of cork and covered with khaki material. We were also issued with two long-john woollen underpants, two long sleeved woollen singlets and several top of the sleeve badges with 'Netherlands East Indies' embroidered on them to replace the 'Netherlands' ones we had been given in Africa. Wolverhampton was a very nice city with very friendly people. Whenever we went into a pub there was always someone there who would pay for our drinks. And there was no way to retaliate. It even became embarrassing at times. We used to go into town every night. Apart from the mess it was the only place where we could find warmth. Since I had learned to

119

dance, me and my mates were going to dance halls nearly every night. There they had some local type dances like the progressive barn dance, the Pride of Erin, the Boston Two Step and the like, dances that we had to adjust to but we soon did. They also had dancing games like musical chairs and others.

One night I was dancing and the game was that every time the music stopped the organiser would call for an item. A white handkerchief or a blue sock or a black fountain pen. If the couples could toss into the basket the items requested they were allowed to continue the dance. The last couple left on the floor would win a prize. That night, at the game, my partner and I were doing pretty well, she was a girl that I had just picked off the wall. When the music stopped again the call this time was for a pair of green knickers. Of course all the other couples left the floor but my girl reached under her dress and produced the item. As you can well imagine, at seventeen years of age there I stood, in the middle of the dance floor while my partner was taking her pants off in front of everybody. The entire dance hall burst into laughter and clapped. Although she did it discreetly I didn't know where to look. We won the prize; some cigarettes for me and a bottle of cheap perfume for her.

A few days later, early one morning, while I was still trying to get over this embarrassing episode the man on the loudspeaker at the camp announced that all Indian Army personnel had to be ready in full battledress and all gear in front of their barracks by 9am. We had no idea what it was all about; nevertheless we did as we were ordered. When the time came, a long line of trucks appeared and we got aboard. We drove for the rest of the day until late afternoon. Because of the overcast sky we had no idea in which direction we were going. Finally, at about four or five in the afternoon we came to a big city which, by looking at different signs, we discovered to be Liverpool. We were taken to a wharf and joined a few thousand other soldiers who were already waiting there to embark. The ship was the *Dominion Monarch*.

# 14

# DOWN TO AUSTRALIA

## NOVEMBER 1944

It was almost dark when we finally climbed the gangway. We were now well and truly in November 1944. As we came aboard we were taken down, and down, and down and down again until there were no more downs to be taken down to. There we were assigned to long tables fitted on both sides with fixed long bench type seats. On top of the tables were piled up a lot of canvas hammocks and life belts. On the deck head were a number of hooks and we were told to choose two to stretch our hammock. There were no bunks on that ship, only hammocks. The forty-four gallon drums, as yet empty had already been strategically positioned here and there for their purpose. The place smelled of hospital disinfectant but it wasn't

122

too bad. By the time we all settled in it was very crowded. We were told where our Emergency Station positions were on deck. It was also stressed that we had to carry our life belts with us at all times and never to forget it.

As soon as the quartermaster left I decided to find my way back to the open deck. It took me quite a while, I got lost a few times but since I made a point of always going up I eventually found myself breathing fresh air again. I looked at the wharf and soldiers were still coming on board. There were still thousands down there waiting to embark. I walked around the deck looking for a private 'spot' like the one I had on the *Eastern Prince*. There were a few possibilities but I would have to wait until we put out to sea before I decided. I asked a few of the crew where we were going and the answer was always 'No idea, mate.'

While we were still at the camp in Wolverhampton the word had got around that the Netherlands East Indies Army did its training in the Belgian Congo. So for the next few days it was generally accepted by us Dutch, that the Congo would be our destination. When I finally went down to sleep I discovered that there were two types of hammocks, some with long ropes and others with short ropes. I also discovered that all the short rope hammocks had been taken and were stretched up high under the deck head. I was left with a long rope hammock. It meant that mine would stretch underneath the short rope ones. A lower layer of hammocks so to speak. I wasn't the only one in the lower layer but I did immediately anticipate what would happen when the sea got rough and those on the top layer of hammocks would suddenly succumb to the impulse of throwing away their breakfast or their dinner. I knew there and then that this wasn't for me. I decided to stay there for the night and to definitely secure myself a 'spot' on deck the next day.

Early next morning, when I got on deck I was surprised to see that soldiers were still boarding and the wharf was still full of trucks disgorging would-be fellow travellers. This went on until late afternoon. An hour or so later we were moving out. We didn't go very far. Like in Algiers we went out and waited for the convoy to be assembled. By then I had found myself a 'spot'. Once again on the outside of a lifeboat, right on the edge of the deck. I was protected from falling overboard, if the sea got rough, by an eight inch or so low bulkhead. No one could see me there and that night I slept very well. The next day was dull and the only significant event was the blasting of the Emergency Station at 10am. This is when I became aware of the huge number of soldiers on board.

The main deck where we were was standing room only, shoulder to shoulder. There were two more, higher decks for officers and various female services personnel and they were pretty well full also from what we could see. These upper decks remained out of bounds to us for the entire voyage. By then I had already decided what my routine would be. I would go down below to collect my food in my mess gear and eat it on deck. I would stay on deck during the day and at nine thirty at night I would go down to get my 'Lime'. This was a special type of thick lime tasting cordial specially doctored with vitamins to prevent us from getting beri beri. After that I would go back on deck, and when most of the 'voyagers' had gone to bed I would reach my 'spot' and peacefully sleep there. On the second night I suddenly woke up. We were on our way. The sea did not appear to be particularly rough but the boat was lurching a bit. I started to think about the Belgian Congo and soon fell asleep again. When I woke up it was daylight but the weather was dull again. I noticed that quite a number of other soldiers had also got themselves a 'spot'. We were in a very large convoy. On both sides there were ships as far as the eye could see. Navy corvettes and destroyers were manoeuvering in and out between the ships. We were armed, not for attack but for defence. On the decks a number of gun towers had been set up. During the Emergency Station that day we had been told that they needed volunteers to help the Navy man these towers, particularly at night.

We were also told that if we were torpedoed to make sure we got out of the water within fifteen minutes, 'because in twenty minutes you're dead. Swim your way to one of the rafts as quickly as you can.' As if we had to be convinced by someone else to do just that. Particularly in freezing water that kills you in twenty minutes. The rafts were something which had taken our attention as we came on board. There were a lot of lifeboats on the ship but obviously not enough to cater for the thousands of personnel now on board. Huge big stacks of rafts had been piled in different places to complement the lifeboats in case of emergency. They were large square rafts painted red, about nine feet by nine feet (about 2.8 metres) with hold on ropes all the way around. They had no up or down side. They were functional whichever way they hit the water.

We also had had some on the *Eastern Prince* when we came from Algiers. Although I never had to use any of them they looked effective enough. A few days on our way, the sea became

125

terribly rough and the weather very bad and very cold. At night the spray from the sea would turn immediately to ice. In my 'spot' there were a number of coils of rope and I used them to protect myself from it. I would pull my great coat over my head and I wasn't cold.

One day at one of the Emergency Station round-ups, I volunteered for a night duty on the gun towers. I really only wanted to see what it was like. I was told where to go and at sunset I fronted up. Another soldier, an Englishman, showed up as well. The tower was a five feet, round vertical column about ten feet (about 3 metres) high. On top was a circular platform about fifteen feet in diameter with a gun in the middle and protected all around with a four feet (about 1.2 metre) high armed plate.

When we got on top we were issued with a helmet, a duffel coat, a long pair of white hand-knitted woollen stockings and a pair of rubber gum boots. I put on the helmet, the duffel coat and the boots but I didn't bother about the stockings. I was used to sleeping on deck with every bit of clothing I owned under my battle dress so I wasn't really cold. There were four Royal Navy sailors there to man the gun. Our job would have been to pass on ammunition to one of the sailors when the firing started, but it didn't. There was no firing. It turned out to be an uneventful night relieved at times by hot mugs of cocoa, sandwiches and tea.

During Emergency Station one morning, we were told our future address: 'For those of you who have something to write it down, it is Netherlands East Indies Army, Camp Columbia Wacol, Brisbane.'

As soon as the Emergency Station was blasted off we all rushed to the library for a map of the Belgian Congo. We couldn't find Brisbane on it. We thought that it might have been such a small place that it wouldn't even figure on the map of the Belgian Congo. Then someone said 'The only Brisbane I've heard of is somewhere in Australia.' It was only a few days later when the weather fined up and we could see the sun that we noticed that we were going North West and that therefore we could kiss the Belgian Congo goodbye.

Now we knew where we were going. The largest part of the 'voyagers' on the *Dominion Monarch* were English servicemen and women, Army, Navy and Air Force. Then came us, the Dutch, and a few Australian soldiers but not many. One afternoon, on deck, I was talking to a Dutch soldier I knew. His name was Jan Van Koefaring. I told him about my 'spot' and he told me that he had a cabin. He said that in civilian life he was a baker and that he had volunteered to help in the bakery and so he was given a bunk in a four-bunk cabin to sleep during the day. He told me that I could volunteer as well because they could use as many men as wanted to be in it.

That night after dinner I fronted up at the bakery with my friend. I was taken to a store by one of the crew bakers and for the next hour or so all I did was to bring bags of flour to the bakery. The bakery was in fact a part of the huge galley. When finally they had enough flour I was made to join the other bakers at a stainless steel top bench to knead the dough. The pieces of dough were cut to size by one of the ship's bakers and all we had to do was to knead them into a ball and toss them into a bread tin. The bread tins were then put into steel cupboards with steam coming out of the walls to make the dough rise. Later, the tins were placed in a conveying oven whence they would come out at the other end full of beautifully cooked bread loaves. We used to bake six thousand loaves of bread per night. Plus a few thousands bread rolls. These were made on a machine. The dough was rolled flat, like a pizza, and then placed on top of a round machine and covered with a lid. When turned on the machine would vibrate and when the lid was lifted there were dozens of little balls of dough ready for the oven. The best part came at about 1am. The butchers and the pastry cooks would come over and start their shift. First came night time lunch. The butchers would cut and cook beautiful pieces of meat and with fresh bread and butter it was a delight. For dessert there was always cake and custard or tinned fruits. After that we would empty the bread tins and stack the bread in baskets.

By four or five we were finished. I also had been given a bunk in a cabin to sleep it off for the rest of the day. Sometimes when I woke up in the afternoon I would go on deck. By then we were in the North Atlantic. We were going very slowly, our speed would not have been more than about four knots. We had to keep to the speed of the slowest ships in the convoy. The sea was always unbelievably rough. About three hundred yards to starboard was a Royal Navy destroyer, the sea was so bad that at times it would completely disappear in the low of a wave. Although it was expected at any time, we were never attacked by submarines.

This went on for about a month. One morning we noticed that the rest of the convoy had disappeared and that we were on our own. We also noticed that we were now going a lot faster and that we were heading south-west. Gradually over the next few days the weather and the temperature began to improve. One night, a week or so later, while we were making bread, we heard the anchor chain drop. Later, when the butchers and the pastry cooks came to start their shift, they told us that we were in Cristobal. At the mouth of the Panama Canal.

The following morning we berthed at a wharf but we were not allowed to go ashore. That afternoon however we were invited to a show put on by the USO. It was arranged in one of the large stores across the wharf right opposite the ship. We were treated to a professional performance by well-known artists, accompanied by a large band. It was a salutary contribution to our morale. I for one thought that we were going so far that there was no chance in hell that I would ever see Europe again. In those days the world was big and Australia was on the other side of it. None of us knew anything about Australia. The USO company performed three shows. By midnight all those on board who wanted to attend had seen one of the performances.

The next morning I didn't go to bed. When we were finished in the bakery I went on deck. We were already being manoeuvred to access the Canal. By the time we reached the first lock there was standing room only on deck. I was marvellously impressed by this majestic piece of engineering achievement. We were being towed from one lock to the next by small diesel locomotives on each side of the lock. The word got around that the *Dominion Monarch* was the largest ship that ever went through the Canal, It wasn't the first time that it went through but it was, at that time, the largest that ever did.

When we got up to Lake Gatum we proceeded on our own power. A couple of banana boats hooked themselves alongside and were selling us bunches. I was given some—I had not seen a banana since the war had started. Late that afternoon we reached the other end of the lake, and we went down the locks to sea level again. As night fell we were sailing alone, without convoy or escort, into the Pacific Ocean. That night I gave my bread-making job away and returned to my 'spot'. By then it was summer and I didn't need the cabin anymore.

The voyage was like a cruise. We were going a lot faster now. At least four times faster than our cruising speed in the convoy. The weather was fine, the sea was calm and most of the soldiers were becoming better sailors. Every time I went down I noticed that the forty-four gallon drums were not as full as they had been when we were cruising in the North Atlantic. We were now in the Tropics. On deck the English boys, stripped to their waists, were sunbathing. Like a bunch of chameleons, most of them were changing colour every day. They began white as sheets, as white as the skin of an Englishman can be. The next day they would be bright red, like a boiled lobster and the day after that they would be blue all over. That was the colour of the lotion dispensed at the infirmary to those who had overdone it.

When we reached the Equator the traditional, stupid pranks prevailed during the entire afternoon. I kept well away from the enthusiasts and was spared the ridiculous sacerdotal introduction to the Southern Hemisphere. Except for that so called memorable Investiture to the other side of the world, and that we were now in 1945, the rest of the trip went on without any spectacular event.

One morning we were told that we would reach our destination later that afternoon. It was to be Sydney. That day, after lunch, I made my way as close as I could to the bow of the ship to be one of the first to witness landfall. By about 4 p.m. I could see land right across the horizon. An hour later it became a lot clearer but all I could see were sand dunes. We seemed to be going straight to them. There were no signs of habitation, only sand. My most unimpressed vision of our destination was interrupted by the dinner bell. I went down to get my dinner and passed onto my mates my first impressions of Sydney.

'It must be a real dump. Probably just a bunch of huts. No I didn't see anybody on the land.' We had our meal and by then we could feel that the ship had stopped. After dinner, some of us decided to go on deck for a breath of fresh air. We had the shock of our lives. There we were, moored at Circular Quay. In the sky behind us was the formidable shadow of the Harbour Bridge, all lit up. There was no curfew in Sydney. The city was all lights and traffic and trams. Alongside of us ferryboats were cruising across the harbour. We were flabbergasted. Particularly after my initial impression and rendering of what I thought the city would be like.

We slept on board that night. The next morning we were told that we could leave the ship and return again that night to sleep on board, or that we could have the day and the night off. I don't think any one accepted the first offer. I certainly didn't. Those of us who chose to have the night off were told to report the following evening at the entrance to Central Station. We didn't know where it was but we knew that we had thirty-six hours to find it.

# 15

# CAMP COLUMBIA, BRISBANE

## FEBRUARY 1945

With two of my friends from Algiers, Eddie Eidenberg and Jan Den Hartog we found a place to leave our kitbags and walked and rode trams all day around Sydney. We wanted to familiarise ourselves with this beautiful city. We drank milk shakes until they were coming out of our ears. We flirted without success with every girl we passed in the streets, and that night we finished up in the YMCA at the top of Pitt Street. The next day we checked out but left our gear at the Y to be picked up in the afternoon. We went to Luna Park across the harbour then back to Circular Quay; we took another ferry to Manly. We didn't swim but we had a very good time. That night by 6pm we were at Central with our kitbags. We were all marched to a platform inside the station. There were a lot of soldiers there already waiting, mostly Australians and a few Americans. There, for the first time, we also saw what our new enemy looked like. About a dozen or fifteen Japanese prisoners of war were waiting under guard to board a train on the other side of the platform. They were a miserable looking bunch with POW painted in white on the back of their Australian tunics and on the front of their trousers.

Our train pulled into the station backwards and we were assigned to a carriage. Inside, each of us had a bunk. Very comfortable. It must have been a hospital train. At each end of the carriage was a small balcony which reminded us of the trains we saw in cowboy films. We were told that we were going to Brisbane. We organised ourselves as best we could, there were three rows of bunks super-imposed on each side of the carriage and this time I took a top one. We had no idea how far Brisbane was from Sydney.

We travelled the whole of that night, the whole of the following day and half of the day after that. In fact we did more stopping than travelling. We would stop at a siding for hours waiting for a train to come the other way. Then we would go on again for a couple of hours and stop again and wait. We were anxious to get there but otherwise there was nothing wrong with the delays. We were extremely comfortable. We could lie down and read or sleep whenever we felt like it. For our meals we would stop at some small country railway station and there, wonderful food and tea was waiting for us.

What we were short of was water. At both ends of the carriage, in a large round bracket was a huge water carafe which was refilled at every food stop. The intention was noble but unfortunately inadequate. It was summer, it was hot, and it wasn't enough. We were thirsty. We relied mostly on our canteens but even with that we were always thirsty. At the stops there was always a tap or two where we could refill our canteens, unfortunately there were always too many of us wanting to do the same thing. You have no idea how long it takes to fill a canteen at a water tap. I missed out a few times.

Eventually we came to our final stop. To us it was meant to be Brisbane. It was a siding to the side of a very small open shelter. From where I was, I could not see the name of it, although it must have been written somewhere. A few trucks were there waiting for us Dutch. The other soldiers remained on the train. We boarded the trucks and looked in dismay at each other. Brisbane somehow appeared to be quite different from Sydney. We drove from what I now think must have been somewhere near Coopers Plains to Wacol Station. There we crossed another railway line and straight after that, on the right hand side, was Camp Columbia. It was mid-January 1945. Columbia was a Netherlands East Indies Army Headquarters and sorting camp. The camp contained native soldiers from the Dutch East Indies and white European Dutchmen in the KNIL. From there Dutch and native soldiers were sent to different units stationed either in Australia, New Guinea or some other islands in the Pacific.

We got off the trucks and were assigned to very spacious barracks. We were also given the rest of the day off. We showered and shaved and went for lunch. The camp had two messes, one where European food was dished out and another where the Indians, as the natives of the Dutch East Indies were called, were served their own type of food. It looked very good. There were two or three European Dutch here and there, also lining up in the Indian queue. After all these weeks I was somewhat sick of roasted meat and three vegetables, so I decided to change queues. When my turn came an Indian cook filled my mess gear with rice and offered me several kinds of stewed meat to have with it. It looked delicious. I selected a couple of helpings and passed on to the next one. He was serving two quarters of a green orange and a nice thick bright red tomato sauce which he was dishing out in very small amounts on the edge of the rice.

I liked tomato sauce and this one looked extremely appetising. Before the war at home my mother used a lot of it with boiled rice, it was delicious. When the man started to dish out his small helping of tomato sauce I asked for more and he gave me more. But I wanted more again and I got more and then I asked him to cover the rice with it and he did and he laughed and all the Indians queuing up behind me also laughed. Idiots! I proceeded to a table and set out to eat my lunch while all the other Indians instead of getting stuck into their meals were looking at me with a stupid smile on their faces. I didn't care and got stuck into mine. I took a great big mouthful of tomato rice into my mouth.

Oh boy! Oh boy! ... that tomato sauce! Oh boy! Help! Help! It was chilli paste. Now I knew why they were laughing. But of course smart Alec me, the show off, I couldn't lose face in front of the boys. So I went on as if it was the sort of stuff I ate everyday; somehow I ate the bloody lot in front of them. Easing the pain from time to time by biting into the green orange quarters.

The rest of the afternoon I spent quenching my mouth, settling in and speculating as to where I was likely to be posted. Before we left Wolverhampton I, and a few others who at school, had passed the leaving certificate had been told that we were to undergo an officers' training course. We had no idea where but obviously it wasn't going to be in the Belgian Congo.

That evening some of us managed to get a lift into town. There were trucks going to town every evening and coming back at midnight. The trucks went as far as Woollongabba and stopped there, about twelve miles away. We got off there and were quite impressed with Brisbane town. It was more than what we had expected. There was a pub on the main corner and a couple of cafés and shops. There was even a stadium across the street. It wasn't too bad. It was certainly better than the place where we had got off the train. At least it looked like a town with solid buildings.

It was the following evening that, exploring on foot, we discovered South Brisbane. It had a railway station with a long air raid shelter in front of it slightly to the left, and a couple of pubs and cafés. Even a theatre and a Chinese restaurant. We were impressed. We saw the Victoria Bridge by the river but there was no point going across it. Since the Railway station was here this had to be the centre of Brisbane.

The next day we were told that all the trains from Wacol Station went into Brisbane. That evening instead of going by truck a few of the boys and I went to the Railway Station.

When we got there over a thousand soldiers were waiting for the train. They were mostly Americans from a huge army camp situated right across the main road from us. That night we really discovered Brisbane. The train went to Roma Street Station. That was really Brisbane. It wasn't a town it was a city. A big and beautiful city with all the amenities that a large city has to offer. The greatest appeal of course, for us soldiers, was the City Hall. There was dancing there every night until 11.30. It was always full and the music was great. It was patronised mainly by men and women in uniform, Americans, Australians and Dutch. But there were also a few civilians, ordinary Brisbane boys and girls.

After 11.30, when the dancing stopped we would walk over to the Albert Park at the back of the Railway Station for a kiss and a cuddle. It was always crowded. It was difficult to find a place on the grass to sit. At midnight the last train would leave the Station and if we missed it we had to wait for the next one at 6am. When we did miss it, we would go back to the park and talk and smoke and tell jokes for the rest of the night with all the other soldiers who had also missed the last train. And there were always hundreds of them. I stayed at Camp Columbia a few days.

One morning a Sergeant Major came into our barracks and called out some of our names and where we were assigned to. I was to go to Camp Victory at Casino. Camp Colombia was in Queensland, Casino was over the border in New South Wales. Those of us assigned to Camp Victory were to be taken there by truck the next day. Those going to Melbourne were to go by train from South Brisbane. That day we were outfitted with our new uniforms and given a .303 rifle. Except for the English helmet and ammunition pouches, the uniforms were American.

The trip to Casino was spectacular. The scenery was unbelievable. We went through jungle and rain forests. It was the type of landscape that I had never seen before. There was nothing like that in France and even in the part of Africa where I had been everything had been barren and dry. This was fresh and moist and beautiful. Camp Victory was a huge big tent camp. There were a few barracks for offices and amenities but the men lived in tents. The big square American tents with a centre pole. Like the ones we had in Algiers. The camp held the First Battalion of Netherlands East Indies Infantry. It was made up mainly of what we now call Indonesians. They were all professional soldiers from the Nederlandsch Indisch Leger which had been the army in the Dutch East Indies before the Japanese invasion. They had last fought in Timor with the Australians before being evacuated to Australia in 1942. Now they were used in different theatres of war under General MacArthur.

I was assigned to the First Battalion commanded by Colonel Breemaurer. I joined the First Platoon of the Fourth Company under Captain Lewtein. I shared a tent with three other men who had come with me from Brisbane. Our Section was made up of raw recruits; men who had never had a gun in their hands before. When it became obvious that I had had combat experience I was told to report to Captain Lewtein. He told me that we were all earmarked for officer's training. He said the others had to have some kind of basic training first but since that did not apply to me I was to go to Seymour in Victoria to start my training immediately at the start of the next course. He also told me that

I had to learn to speak Malay as soon as possible because most of the soldiers did not speak Dutch they only understood the commands in Dutch but nothing else. He told me that Malay was easy to learn and he gave me a book to study.

The next course turned out to be in less than a week later. I was given a rail pass and travelled all the way to Sydney and then on to Seymour by myself. I arrived on a Sunday afternoon. I was picked up at the station by an Australian Sergeant and taken by jeep to what was called The Junior Leader School. It was just a few miles out of town. There I reported to the office. I was told where to go and was also given a couple of pages of typed instructions to memorise. After a determined search I eventually found my tent. I was the only one there. It was as yet unoccupied. While settling in, five other Dutch soldiers appeared. They had just arrived from Melbourne. Three shared my tent and two went next door. We were to do the course together. It was the very beginning of February 1945.

The next morning at 6am, reveille was bugled over the loud speakers. After that, loud music came over the air to keep us awake. Even though it was early February, at 6am it was fairly cool. As per our sheets of instructions, half an hour later we had to attend sick parade. That meant sick or not sick we had to front up. After that, breakfast and then fall in for the day. A break for lunch and a break for dinner. The food was good and plentiful. At night, after dinner, it was military theory, in a barrack, until 10pm. By then it was time for a visit to the canteen where we could buy a beer and a hot dog and after that straight to bed. They were very full days, being young and keen we didn't mind. We had Saturday nights and Sundays off.

139

The town of Seymour was just a big army base. Even most of the civilians there were attached to the army in one way or another. There were three large army bases around Seymour; Pukapunyal, OCTU (Officers Corp Training Unit) and the Junior Leader School where I was. Saturday nights we usually spent at a dance or at the cinema and Sunday was spent studying or revising. We had been told that in order to be able to pursue our officer training we had to be within the first ten of our group to qualify. I didn't think this was quite fair. The lectures were in English. It didn't matter to me or to Jerry Lemmens who came from Melbourne where he and his family had lived after escaping from the Dutch East Indies when the Japs took over. Unfortunately the other Dutch boys did not speak English too well. Yet it was expected that they should come well ahead of most of the Australians doing the same course.

The weeks at the Junior Leader School were spent training and using different types of weapons. We learned to find places using compass headings, sometimes at night. We learned how to use flame-throwers and flares, how to drive various army vehicles including Bren Carriers. These were a small tank type vehicle open on top, powered by a Ford V8 engine and driven with a steering wheel instead of levers. Great emphasis was made on the use of heavy infantry weapons like the Vickers machine gun and the three-inch mortar. We learned to throw hand grenades and how to fire them from a rifle using a special pot which could be attached to the muzzle of the rifle and the grenade ejected using a special ballistic cartridge which had no bullet.

The theory classes at night were also very interesting. We were taught the basics of navigation in bad weather using only a compass; some principles of trajectory, which also applied to the three-inch mortar and various behavioural practices to be adopted in front line circumstances. It was in these lectures that I realised the importance given by the real army to the preservation of human life. The primordial duty for a leader is not to endanger the life of his men in puerile acts of bravado but to assess risks and evaluate casualty cost before giving an order. I couldn't help thinking back to the *Maquis* days when 'guts' and plenty of it was wasted by courageous but inexperienced leaders. They meant well but they squandered young human lives in pointless exercises, which led nowhere and gave no benefits.

A payday came and we were told to line up with the Australians to get our pay. We were by then incorporated in the 2nd Australian Imperial Forces based in Seymour. As my turn came to be paid the paymaster started to dish out quite a number of pound notes. A Colonel standing by saw this and in a friendly voice said to me, 'A bit of back pay eh?' I was stupid enough to say, 'No Sir, that's what we get every time.' The old Colonel became enraged and shouted at the top of his voice, 'I shall not have that. While you chaps are here with us you will get the same as the others.' The way he said it did not invite discussion so I said nothing.

The course lasted just under three weeks. We had an exam and all six of us passed; all of us within the first ten. After that we all thought that our next stop would be O.C.T.U; we were wrong. I don't remember where the other five were sent to but I was given a rail pass to Brisbane and told to report to Camp Columbia. That was early March 1945.

# 16

# NEW GUINEA AND BACK

## MARCH 1945

After an excruciatingly long trip I arrived at South Brisbane Station. There, with my kitbag on my shoulder I walked across the Grey Street Bridge to Roma Street Station and took a train to Wacol.

When I reported at the Headquarters I was told that the Commanding Officer wanted to see me. After waiting for a while in the lobby I was sent to his office.

He stood up, shook my hand and congratulated me for now being a sergeant. This time, not only for being able to speak English but for being an expert at my job as a soldier. He also gave me an envelope which contained my brass bars to be fitted on my epaulettes.

The following day I was ordered to report to H.Q. again. This time I was told where I was being sent to: Hollandia, north New Guinea. I was also given an envelope that I was to hand over to the Commanding Officer of the Dutch contingent there.

In the afternoon I was taken by jeep to Archerfield aerodrome. There, amongst others was based the 18th Squadron KNIL Air Transport. I had dinner there and slept the night on a camp stretcher on the ground floor of the tower building. The next morning, after breakfast, two pilots picked me up and we went to a B25 bomber, which had been transformed into a transport plane with a large double door on the port side. It was fully loaded with crates of engine parts but there were also a lot of crates of vegetables and Coca-Cola. We took off almost immediately. At first I sat on some of the crates and later I went to the back of the cockpit so I could speak to the pilots.

Early in the afternoon we came down and landed at a place called Batchelor. We were in the Northern Territory. For the two pilots who had taken me there it was the end of the trip. Not for me; I had something to eat in a kind of canteen and immediately after I boarded another Mitchell Bomber. This one had also been set up as a transport plane. Inside were a few crates and a few airplane tyres but it was not full. I was still the only passenger in the plane. We took off and again I went and sat at the rear of the cockpit so that I could again speak to the pilots. Before long we were flying over the sea. A couple of hours later we landed on a dirt strip. I thought this was Hollandia but the pilots told me that it was Merauke, on the south coast of New Guinea. There we unloaded the crates but not the tyres. We refuelled and took on board about eighteen native Dutch East Indies soldiers. We waited until it got dark and we took off. Our next stop now was to be Hollandia on the north coast.

That night flight was an experience. Soon after we took off, we were being shot at by anti-aircraft guns. There were no searchlights only gunfire. The night was moonlit and quite clear, they probably could see our plane but the firing was far from being accurate. The pilots were laughing and joking about it and they certainly did not alter our course because of the firing. The Indian soldiers, sitting here and there and on the deck did not blink an eyelid. They seemed quite resigned to it. Within a few minutes the shooting stopped, we were out of range. In the moonlight I could see huge mountains, they seemed very steep, with dark deep ravines in between. From the air it appeared quite inhospitable terrain.

Later during the night we again passed over areas which had anti-aircraft guns and they fired at us, again with no effect. It was daybreak when we reached Hollandia. I was surprised how big it was. From the air I could see large camps, and many barracks. A harbour full of ships of all kinds. There was one cruiser there and a few destroyers and LSTs. The aerodrome had planes everywhere. One of the pilots told me that General MacArthur had his Headquarters there until just recently.

We circled a couple of times and then we got permission to land. There waiting for us were a few army trucks. We boarded the trucks and were taken to a camp. We did what seemed a lot of driving but in fact our camp was well within the military complex. I was directed to a tent where I met two sergeant majors. They were Dutch. While I was talking to them another sergeant major walked in. It was Willy Hogerslag, the friend with whom I had shared a tent in Algiers and with whom I had gone into the dance hall in London where I first learned to dance. I do not remember the names of the other two Sergeant Majors but I was very pleased to meet with Willy again. In the afternoon I reported to the Commanding Officer. I have a bad memory for names except for those with whom I have had close contact. But I think his name was Captain Verschrouer. He was tall and thick but not fat. His most outstanding feature was the way he tilted his head forward and to the side when he talked to me, as if he could hear better from one ear rather than the other. I gave him the envelope I had with me. He read whatever was in it and said that he knew that I was undergoing Officer's training in Victoria and that I was there for only a short time for field practice. He told me that he had also been at the OCTU in Seymour and that it was there that he had first got his commission.

He asked me what I thought of it or words to that effect. My answer was that I had only just finished Junior Leader and that OCTU, for me, was yet to come. He told me that New Guinea was almost completely liberated. According to him, Australian New Guinea was now totally free, but inland Dutch New Guinea there were some pockets of Japanese Forces which were still active in guerilla type warfare. Our duty there, from what he said, was to go and patrol certain areas inland where natives had reported the presence of Japanese soldiers. When I told him that I had already met Willy and that Willy and I went all the way back to Algiers he assigned me to Sergeant Major Hogerslag's platoon.

145

We left camp after breakfast the next day in three GMC trucks. Hogerslag's platoon was made up of three Sections and a small Commando Group, altogether about forty men. We drove for hours on roads that were little more than foot-tracks. At about lunchtime we stopped and the cooks cooked some rice. For lunch we had boiled rice and a tin of sardines each. As time went on and in subsequent similar conditions elsewhere I discovered that, although we were issued with American K rations, rice and sardines was the staple diet of the Dutch East Indies Army infantry in combat conditions. Probably due to the fact that most of the soldiers were Muslims.

After lunch the trucks went back and we started on our patrol. Willy was a professional and experienced soldier. Before we moved he called me over and showed me on a map where we had to go and what area we had to patrol. We were about thirty miles south west of Mount Cyclop. From there our itinerary was almost due west for about twenty miles (about 32 kilometres) and then north to the coast where we would be picked up again near a small village. I was second in command under Willy, which meant that if anything happened to him I was to take over. Each Section of the platoon was commanded by a corporal, who was an East Indies Dutchman. Willy and I were the only two Europeans.

Before we started walking we took a 260 degree bearing on the top of a mountain on the other side of the ravine. One could not possibly call that a valley, it was more like a gorge. It was hot and steep. There were a lot of trees but no jungle. The going was slow. As we were going down we had to take new intermediate bearings because we lost sight of the one we had

146

originally taken. When we got to the bottom it was rainforest. We came to a fast running creek and we all drank and refilled our canteens. We had special pills to purify water but we didn't use them there. This water was running fast and was clear enough to be trusted. After a short rest we started climbing on the other side. The previous descent was hot and slow but this climbing was worse. We kept in line with our intermediate bearings to keep our heading straight and eventually our original destination came into sight again.

By the time we got there it was almost dark and we made camp for the night. The boys proceeded to light a fire and Willy told me that it was safe enough. He assigned one of the corporals to organise a watch for the night. We sat down and looked at the map. We had done a lot of walking but we hadn't gone very far on the map. Tomorrow would be the real test. The dinner was the same as our lunch, rice and sardines. One of the corporals brought Willy and I some chillies that he had brought with him. The difference the addition of these little red condiments made to our rice was unbelievable. After dinner we fell asleep on the grass where we stood. I thought that we might have had trouble with mosquitoes but we didn't. There were a few, but not enough to be a pest. We were too high for that.

The next day was more of the same as we had had the previous afternoon. Down ravines and up mountains. We were looking for Japanese soldiers but as Willy had said the only way to find them is to let them find us. The idea was to entice the Japs to attack us and pass on their position so that the Air Force could blast them out of the jungle. That night we slept in the open again and by late afternoon the following day we were being picked up by the trucks and taken back to the camp. We had the next day off and I stayed on my camp stretcher most of the day. That night Willy told me that we were on again the next morning. As before, we left by truck and drove along the coast past where we had been picked up last time and then south into the interior. Again at about lunch time the trucks stopped and we were on our own. We had our rice and sardines and started on our patrol. This time the going wasn't too bad but when we took our bearing I saw that we would end up at the top of what looked like a very high mountain. Our tactic was the same as before, look for Japs and let them find us. And that day again they did not find us. At sunset we made camp had a meal and enjoyed a nice cool night.

The next morning, after breakfast, we resumed our track; this time slightly more south-west. We seemed to be on a plateau or at least we were following the ridges. At lunchtime Willy called for a stop and we did. We each found a spot in the shade and lay down. As I was lying down with my hands under the back of my head and my legs crossed in the air there was a huge explosion. I felt a sharp pain in my left foot. I knew I had been hit. I thought the Japs had finally found us but when I sat up and turned around I saw what had happened. One of the soldiers had been blown to pieces. Apparently he had been in the process of taking off his harness when a hand grenade in his pouch had blown up and blown the others with it. The 'spoon' in the grenade, which keeps the plunger off the detonator, is secured with a split pin fitted to a ring. When first issued the ends of the split pin are bent over slightly to prevent it from slipping out accidentally while handling. But because it is quite an effort to pull the pin out when its ends are bent over a lot of the boys used to straighten the ends of the pin somewhat to make it easier to pull.

I had never seen or heard of a pin falling out by itself but this is what had obviously happened. Luckily he was a fair distance away from us probably looking for a spot to do an intimate job. Of course he was killed on the spot. A few of the men were holding on to different parts of their limbs but none of them appeared to be seriously affected.

By then my foot didn't hurt anymore but the toe part of my shoe was smashed. I thought I'd better take my shoe off and have a look at my foot and that is when it started to hurt again. When I finally managed to take my shoe off I saw that my big toe was smashed flat. It looked as if it had been placed on an anvil and someone had hit it with a sledge hammer. It wasn't bleeding very much nor was it very sore but it looked disgusting. I covered it with sulphanilamide powder that I had in my medical kit and made a tight dressing. I was asked a couple of times if I needed help but I refused. Most of the men were tending to the few others who had been slightly hurt. There were a few torn shirts and trousers with scratches underneath, but no real blood. No one had been seriously hurt. Apart from the poor devil who had been killed, my toe was the most serious injury and in reality it was nothing.

Of course I could not put my shoe back on with the thick dressing on my toe so I decided to cut out the front part of my left shoe. The only things I had with me which looked at all suitable were my machete and my bayonet. I tried to use them but they were both too blunt. In all my time in the army I have

149

never myself, nor seen anyone else, ever sharpen a bayonet. Although we used to practice with it quite a lot most of us knew that hand-to-hand combat with bayonets had ended with the First World War. Nevertheless there I was, and I had to cut off part of my shoe. My machete and my bayonet, as they were, were certainly not going to do it. Those army shoes were like a type of desert boot; very soft and made of thick suede leather. I asked around but no one else had a suitable knife. In the end I put my bayonet in the fire until it got red hot and used it to burn through the shoe. It stank a lot but it worked quite well. Instead of going on with the patrol Willy decided to return to camp. He sent one of the corporals and a man ahead to get the trucks back where they had left us. This time we walked non-stop. Although a good part of my left shoe was missing I could walk quite well and it wasn't very sore. At times it did hurt but I kept taking aspirins.

By daybreak we finally saw the trucks. They had been alerted and they were there waiting for us. By late morning we were back at the camp. Those of us who had been hurt were told to stay on the truck to be taken to the American hospital. I didn't go. I thought I might be needed to write some kind of report about the incident. The matter was discussed with Willy and he wrote the report. After that he told me to go to the hospital but I refused. I didn't think that the injury to my foot was serious enough to be hospitalised. I drank some *sopy*, which had been smuggled into our tent and almost immediately my foot felt a lot better. I lay on the bed for the rest of the day. That night I went for dinner, this time it was a real meal, no rice and no sardines.

When it was over I went back to my tent and to the rest of the *sopy*. When Willy came in he touched my forehead and said that I had a temperature. I told him about the *sopy* and he agreed that the jungle juice might have caused it. When I woke up the next morning my foot hurt like hell and even my calf was sore and swollen. Willy got a jeep and took me to the hospital. There an Australian nurse took off my dressing and apparently did not like what she saw. There were little bulges of pus here and there. She went away and later came back with a doctor. He looked at my foot and gave me a needle. I was given more aspirin and taken to a bed. About lunchtime the nurse came to see me and told me that if there was room on the plane tomorrow I would be flown back to Australia. There was room on the plane and the next day I was given a pair of crutches and flown to Darwin and then Townsville in a hospital plane full of sick soldiers.

By then I wasn't feeling well at all. Whenever I stood up to walk with the crutches the pain in my foot became worse and started throbbing. An ambulance took me to one of the barracks where I was given some sandwiches and told to drink a lot of water. A couple of hours later I was picked up by another ambulance. In it were two other Dutch soldiers. They were sitting up, not wounded but sick with some kind of disease.

We were taken to a Dutch plane, which took us to Brisbane. At Archerfield, as we came off the plane, the three of us were made to lie down on stretchers and carried to another ambulance. That one took us on the long drive to Casino. It was still dark when we arrived at Camp Victory. We were taken straight to the hospital. Because I was 'wounded' I was taken to a different branch of the hospital and put to bed by two native orderlies.

And so ended my first field practice in the Pacific Campaign. It was the end of March and still the only Japs I had seen so far were the few POW at Sydney Central Station the day after I arrived in Australia. After I was settled in bed the matron came over to see me. She was a black, big and fat Dutch army career woman from Suriname, Dutch Guyana. She didn't wear whites, she wore an American uniform the same as ours. She was a Lieutenant.

She put a bedpan beside my bed and told me to use it. I laughed and told her that I would enjoy more hearing my intestines blow up rather than to use that bloody gadget. I told her that I could still manage to walk to the toilet and by the dismissive tone I said it no argument ensued.

Later she came back with a doctor. She undid the dressing and they looked at my foot. I didn't exactly know the word for gangrene in Dutch but I had a feeling that it might have been mentioned. When he spoke to me the doctor said that the toe might have to be amputated. I told him that I didn't want to lose my toe because it would put me out of active service and I didn't want that.

At that time, the end of the war was obviously nowhere in sight, and I had more or less decided to make the army my career. With all the thousands of islands yet to be invaded and conquered it looked at the time that even if my life was spared I would die of old age before the war would end. The doctor said that he would have a good look at my foot later in the afternoon.

At about 4pm an orderly came over and we went to the surgery. The doctor had a good look at my toe and said that he might try something but that if it didn't work then he would have to chop it off. I was kind of semi sitting up on the operating table resting on my elbows. He went and washed his hands and put on red rubber gloves. After a lot of local anaesthetic he got into it. At first I didn't want to look, but after a while I did look. I couldn't see much. He was only a young man but he seemed to know what he was doing. He asked me where it happened and I told him. I also told him that it was an accident. After a while I saw him cut a piece off one of those wooden spatulas used for looking into the throat and laid it on my toe. By then my toe was all flat, like a Vienna Schnitzel. I could see the bone sticking up. He placed the little piece of wood between the bone and the flesh of my toe, sprinkled some pink powder all over it and started to dress it up very gently. He looked at me and said, 'I don't know whether this is going to work, at least we've tried … we'll know in a couple of days.'

A couple of days later I was back in the surgery. The doctor looked at my foot again. He didn't appear too enthusiastic when he said, 'Well, let's have a go … this is going to hurt.' He wasn't kidding. He took out the piece of wood and after that I don't know what he did but I stiffened out in pain and stretched out flat on the operating table beating it with both my fists. The pain was unbelievable.

He was making a very tight bandage around my toe and I could feel his hand squeezing it as hard as he could. For about fifteen minutes I could not talk. After a while he said that in a few days he would have another look at it and that he would know then if I would keep my toe or not. He said the dressing would stay there until then. He gave me some pills for the pain and two orderlies took me back to my bed. That night I did not sleep. The pain was steady and fierce. The pills the doctor had given me did not seem to work. There I was on my bed in agony, rolling and tossing with a tiny little bandage on one of my toes while next to me in the ward were men with legs or arms amputated who just lay there motionless and silent. I was ashamed of my reactions but I could not help it.

In the morning, before daylight, the matron brought me a bed-bottle and told me to use it. I told her that I would rather piss the bed than use that. She said, 'If you do you'll stay in it for the rest of the day' and she went on: 'Come on I'll help you if you want.' I was so enraged that I shouted: 'There's no way in the world that I'll let you touch my prick.' She tossed the bottle to me and I tossed it back at her as she was walking away. She didn't look back. She outranked me but in hospital it didn't seem to matter, beside she was a good sort, she took everything said or done as a joke. A few moments later I sat up, picked up my crutches and walked to the toilet. It was agony. I thought I was going to pass out but smart arse me I had to prove it, if not to the matron at least to myself. A few days later, when the doctor finally took off the bandage he smiled. I took it to be a good sign and it was. I looked at it. It looked like a toe except that it did not have a nail on it.

He said laughing, 'Now you can have another go at getting yourself killed.' We laughed but I was pleased. He told me that he qualified as a doctor only a month before the Germans invaded Holland and that he escaped to England just before they came. He was from Maestricht. I told him that I had never lived there but that my family came from there. He told me that he knew because of my name, he said that my family was well known in Maestricht. After that whenever he had a little spare time he would come over and we'd talk. The matron also would often come over and talk. She kept calling me 'Professor' and the other men in the ward would laugh. Although a no nonsense type of woman she was very kind and had a good sense of humour.

Whenever she passed through the ward in a hurry she would call out 'Professor, professor!' and when I turned and looked at her she would raise her hand with the middle finger sticking up. All the boys would laugh and I did too. I made a good friend while I was there. His name was Notokosumo. He was a Prince. His father was a Raja somewhere in Borneo. His bed was opposite mine across the passage. He was not much older than I. He had been wounded and lost a kidney at Aitape in New Guinea. A solid and sophisticated education was obvious in the way he spoke and behaved. We used to play a lot of chess. He told me that he had travelled to Europe with his parents before the war. He had been to Holland and England and France. Not to Marseilles, but to Biarritz, a well known holiday city on the Atlantic south of Bordeaux near the Spanish border.

And so time passed. Army hospital life was just that. Army hospital life! Every day we had a blood test. It was an impromptu performance. The orderly would prick the inside tip of our index finger with a small spring-loaded needle to draw half a drop of blood. Then he would wipe the blood with a piece of blotting paper and run it under a chart, which had different blobs of blood colour on it as a guide. Each blob had a hole cut in its centre and the orderly would estimate your blood count according to which colour your blood matched when he passed the blotting paper under the holes. The entire operation would take the whole of about forty-five seconds.

Our food also was monitored. With our meals, no matter what it was, we had brown rice. Rice with its shell still on it. It was supposed to be a cure for beriberi. It was disgusting. I of course never touched it. It tasted as bad as what I think muesli tastes nowadays. Every day the matron would threaten to ram it down my throat with a stick but she never came around to do it. And by the way, I never did use the bedpan, or the bottle either.

About a week later I was discharged. I still had my toe. It didn't hurt anymore and a sort of nail was attempting to establish itself on it. It looked all right except that instead of growing from south to north it was growing from east to west. As I was getting ready to leave the matron as she was passing my bed shouted, 'Eh professor! Next time you get hit I hope you don't make it here… You've been a real pain in the arse' and they all laughed. I knew she didn't really mean it, it was just her Caribbean sense of humour. I left the hospital barracks and went back to a tent.

# 17

# TARAKAN

## APRIL 1945

When I got to that tent there were two other sergeants billeted there. One of them was Van Koevaring with whom I had made bread with on the *Dominion Monarch*. The other I didn't know. His name was Eitsick. Both of them were also earmarked for officer training. Van Koevaring had not started his course yet but Eitsick had already been at the Junior Leader School in Seymour and, like me, had specialised on the three-inch mortar.

One morning about a week later a sergeant major came to our tent and told Eitsick and I to get ready to leave. There was no point asking him where to for he wouldn't have known anyway. While we were still packing a jeep came to our tent waiting for us. It was the middle of April 1945. We asked the driver where he was taking us to and he said 'Brisbane'. We drove north on the Mount Lindsay Highway and arrived at Camp Columbia at Wacol in mid afternoon. We each found a bed in one of the barracks and reported to the office. We were told that we would be picked up at daybreak the next morning to go to Archerfield aerodrome. The following day, at daybreak, a jeep driven by a KNIL Air Force sergeant pulled up outside our barracks. We were ready to go and we were driven to Archerfield aerodrome. As we arrived there the driver took us straight to a waiting B25 transport plane. A few minutes later we started the same trip as the one I had done not quite two months earlier. Archerfield, Batchelor, Merauke and Hollandia. The Merauke-Hollandia leg again was done at night and we had the same excitement with Japanese anti-aircraft fire.

Eitsick and I were the only two passengers. He had never experienced being shot at in the air before so I was able to reassure him, by now I was a veteran. We landed at Hollandia at first light. There was a jeep waiting for us with a driver and a sergeant major. They did not take us to the Dutch camp. The sergeant major told us that we were to board an American plane very shortly and indeed we did. It was a DC3 troop transport plane and it was full of Yanks. Again we sat on long benches fixed to the sides of the fuselage with our kitbags on the floor in the middle of it. It was an uneventful flight. We refuelled at Biak Island and then flew on to Morotai Island. That was towards the end of April 1945. I had never heard of these islands before. I didn't know they existed. Morotai was a huge big set up; as big as Hollandia if not bigger. There were a lot of Americans there but there were even more Australians. We were taken to a part of the Australian camp where Dutch soldiers

158

were billeted. It was the First Infantry Company of the First Battalion Netherlands East Indies Forces. A contingent of the same Battalion we were part of in Casino but a different company. There we introduced ourselves to the Dutch captain, his name was Nortier. In his mid forties he was a very athletic looking man, with a square jaw and a fireball personality. On that day he was wearing a khaki baseball cap. The meeting wasn't particularly friendly. In fact it was rather abrupt. He knew we were trainee officers but that did not particularly impress him. When I told him that we were both three-inch mortar specialists he said: 'OK, I won't assign you to any platoon but for the time being you will be in the command group.' After this somewhat glacial introduction we were taken to a tent by a sergeant major and we settled in. Life on Morotai was rather hectic. We had heavy training every day in rough terrain with target practice. One day we even had a mock landing on a beach from a landing craft. That night we had a fair idea what we had been sent to this Island for. What we didn't know was when or where.

When turned out to be about a week or so later. One evening as we were queuing up for our dinner we were told to be fully packed up the next morning. That night even though we had not been told where we were to go, we all had a fair idea of what we would be doing when we got there. The next morning we noticed that the Australians had also been told to be ready. They, like us, had no idea what our destination would be but we knew by then that a substantial operation was afoot. We were the only company of Dutch infantry in that camp, about one hundred and forty men or so. We were under the

Command of an Australian Brigadier, I can't remember exactly but I think his name was Whitehouse or Whitehead, something 'White' anyway.

The Australians were by far more numerous. There were over three divisions of them. We were told to assemble on the parade ground and we walked there with our packs. There we waited for an hour or so. At about 10am a number of GMC trucks arrived in small bunches and we were driven to the harbour. There we were taken to a troopship, which was already full of Australian soldiers. As we mixed with the Australians speculation as to our destination was rife. Anything from going back to Sydney to going to land in Tokyo Bay. On that ship we were allowed to stay on deck if we wanted to. That night, while we slept, we got going. The next morning the view of the convoy was spectacular.

As well as troop transports there were a lot of American and Australian warships. There was an Australian cruiser, several Australian and American destroyers and a lot of LSTs and LSIs. Some of the ships had a Landing Craft in tow and so had we. After a couple of days the word went around that we were going to Borneo. That was also Dutch territory. Life on board was rather boring. We were all very excited but there was nothing to do. Nothing to release the tension. We speculated as to what it was going to be like when we finally had to run up the beach. Some of the Australian soldiers had already seen action in Libya and New Guinea but they had never been in a landing. Some of the Dutch soldiers had seen action in Bali and Timor, but neither I nor Eitsick had ever fought a Jap. The tension was rising by the day.

I started to read a book that a man had discarded but after a determined attempt to read it I discarded it also. I couldn't concentrate. We talked about all sorts of things but mainly about girls. We, the Dutch, were also laughing at the yellow Australians. In their dark green battledress their yellow Atabrine skins really stood out. We were also on Atabrine tablets for malaria and just as yellow but our light khaki uniform and the American camouflage overalls that we had been issued with did not contrast as vividly as the dark green outfit of the Australians. After about four days at sea we were called to battle stations in the middle of the night or rather in the early hours of the morning. We knew we had arrived. We were stopped. At first we couldn't see anything. Later, in the distance we could see dark shadows of land sticking out of the sea. It was still dark. At daybreak the warships opened fire. They kept firing non-stop. Some of them were ahead of us much closer to the land. We could see the explosions where the navy shells were landing. On the deck were a lot of boxes of rifle cartridges and crates of hand grenades. We helped ourselves to what we needed. As usual we each took too much. It seems to be a constant preoccupation with soldiers that they are going to run out of ammunition. We always said 'I'll know better next time' but we keep falling for it.

We all stood where our emergency station drill had taken place during the voyage. There we waited. As daylight improved the Australians began to go over the sides into the landing craft. In the distance we could see other ships also unloading their troops in landing craft. As each craft was filled with men they would move away and another craft would take its place. Those already loaded and waiting, were going around in circles. In daylight the land did not seem so far away. There was a lot of smoke there in the distance. The warships were still shelling. When they stopped a large flight of bombers came and dropped bombs everywhere behind the beach.

Eventually our turn came to go over the side. We climbed down to the landing craft by means of a large mesh net secured to the side of the ship. This craft took one platoon of Dutch and all of us in the Command Group. When full we joined the others. By then the bombing had stopped, the planes were gone and we were going towards the land. I don't know what happened to the other two platoons. I didn't see them until later that morning after we had landed. It seemed like ages before we got to the beach but in reality it would have been only about twenty minutes if that. When we landed some of the Australian soldiers were already there. There was no firing. Right at the back of the beach we could see concrete pillboxes sticking out of the ground but there was no firing coming out of them. Before we left the ship the Captain had told us that this was an island called Tarakan and that all we wanted out of it was the airstrip. The fact that no one was firing at us made us feel a little cocky.

As we advanced from the beach we saw a lot of destroyed oil reservoirs. Apparently, before the war, Tarakan had been famous for its oil. We had been told that Tarakan town was a couple of miles inland and the airstrip not much further. We could hear firing in the distance. Obviously the Australians had already engaged the Japs somewhere ahead of us. We Dutch immediately deployed and headed south. As we did we encountered very little Japanese resistance. There was the odd rifle shot but nothing of importance. In the afternoon two Australian Matilda tanks came over to us but there was nothing specifically strategic for them to shoot at so after a while they left and we were on our own again.

That afternoon the Lieutenant of the first platoon told Eitsick and me to report to the Brigadier's Headquarters. Up to then I hadn't fired a shot. We asked the Lieutenant where the Headquarters were and he told us that he had no idea. 'Probably at the port near Lingkas beach' he said. We laughed because he didn't know anymore than we did. He said that the Captain had told him that we would be of better use to the Australians since our company did not have three-inch mortars. Inwardly I felt that it was a good reason to get rid of us. We had a bite to eat and went back towards the beach. Before we got that far we saw a group of four or five Bren Carriers stopped on the side of a road. The crew and the soldiers were having dinner. I sat down with them while Eitsick walked over to a group of Officers talking further up the road.

Shortly after he came back with a lieutenant who immediately assigned us to his unit. To our left a kind of ditch was spouting a lot of black smoke. It probably had been filled with oil and set alight by the Japs. After a while the column started to move and Eitsick and I each climbed aboard a carrier. We went a couple of miles up the road and stopped for the night.

The next morning a detachment of Australian Engineers started clearing the land in front of us. There were mines and booby traps everywhere. As we moved forward one of the carriers struck some kind of a mine. There were no casualties but it blew off several links in the left track. We all stopped. There were more links damaged than the carrier carried as spares so we gave some of ours. I gave a hand to punch out the bent links at one end of the track while others attended the other end. Within half an hour the new links had replaced the broken and twisted ones. The repaired track was laid down flat in front of the vehicle and the carrier slowly proceeded to roll onto it. Five minutes later the two ends of the track were brought together, the links were locked with a pin and we were on our way again.

As we came closer to the airfield Japanese resistance intensified. The Australian infantry was pinned down in front of us. The strip itself was pocked all over by bomb craters. The Japs had good cover and so did we. The Vickers machine guns that we were carrying were unloaded and set up by their crew. We left them there and drove to a small ridge a few hundred yards further. There we took cover behind the ridge and assembled our three-inch mortars. We were three units. The Lieutenant in charge took position at the top of the ridge, relayed the bearings to us, and we began to fire. Eitsick was with another unit. It wasn't long before the Japs had guessed where we were and started to retaliate with their own mortar fire. We fired onto different positions throughout the day. Two of the carriers were sent back for more ammunition and supplies.

At one stage we were given a bearing on a kind of ravine in front of a hill on the other side of the airfield that we could see from our position. To reach it we had to increase the ballistics of our bombs with extra sachets of explosives secured between the fins with rubber bands. From the congratulatory hand sign we got from the Lieutenant after only three or four shells, it must have done the trick. We had the correct distance and bearing. The taking of the airfield did not turn out to be the piece of cake that we all had expected. The somewhat unopposed landing had obviously given us a distorted opinion of what lay ahead. It took four days before the airfield came into our hands. And when it did it sure didn't seem worth the effort. It was completely destroyed. The fighting had been constant and heavy. A lot of Matilda tanks had been used and had done a great job. So did a squadron of bombers with napalm-type bombs. I have no idea how many men the infantry had lost but in our mortar units there were no casualties.

By then we were due for a break. We were relieved by another unit. We drove back toward Lingkas and stopped at Tarakan town. Apparently it had only fallen into our hands the day before even though there had been fighting there since the first day of the landing. As well as local natives in town there were also some Japanese civilians. The Australians had the matter well in hand and were gathering them up. We were exhausted and enjoyed the break. There, all we had to do was to lay down and relax. Just relax.

In the afternoon I spoke to a Dutch sergeant who came into town with a jeep. He had a native soldier with him. He told me that the First Company was still heading south through heavily timbered country against very little opposition. He seemed to think that the Japs had completely given up which certainly wasn't the case around the airstrip. When we moved again, we seemed to be going north. I wasn't really sure and didn't really care. We were following the leading carrier where the

Lieutenant was. Before long we caught up with Australian troops going in the same direction. This time we were going uphill. After a while we left the road and took to the forest. It was timbered but we could still drive the carriers through it. Soon we came to a ridge, which was almost clear. We took position just down a bit from the top and we waited. Over the ridge, slightly down from where we were, the infantry had engaged the Japs. We could hear the firing going on but we could not see anything.

The lieutenant (I can't remember his name but Travis or some like name rings a bell) went to the top. When he came back he ordered the machine gunners to go down and set themselves up on the down slopes We, in the carriers, moved to another position further along and set up our battery. Eitsick as before was with another unit. We were there about three days. While there we moved around a lot to different positions but still in the same sector. During the days, Australian and American airforce planes were bombing the Japs' positions; again with napalm-type bombs.

Eventually the Japs decamped and the firing stopped. We stayed there another day while the infantry was securing the area and then we went back to the town for a well-earned rest. By then I was seriously afflicted by dysentery. Quite a few of us were. We blamed the water. We had special pills to put in our canteens to purify the water but it did not always work. I was passing blood, so was Eitsick and a few of the others. During our rest period I visited the Australian sick bay and was given some tablets to take. They did not seem to work too well but at least I had the feeling that I was doing something about it. It

166

wasn't painful but terribly inconvenient. After a few days we were getting ready to move out again. Our dysentery problem had not really improved, in fact, by then, more of the men in our group were afflicted with it. That morning the Lieutenant told Eitsick and me and a few other men to report to the Quartermaster at Lingkas Harbour.

We managed to get a lift with a couple of ambulances, which were going there. At the harbour the Quartermaster told us to get our gear together and that we were being sent back to Morotai. I could not find my kitbag and I don't think that Eitsick could find his either. That afternoon we boarded an American LST with quite a number of other soldiers, some wounded but most of them sick, many of them with dysentery. We sailed away almost immediately, Eitsick and I without our kitbags. Three days later we were back in Morotai. We were all taken to a hospital but by then our affliction had greatly improved. Two days later an American plane took us and some wounded and sick Australian soldiers to Hollandia. The next day we were back in Brisbane at Camp Columbia. We had been away just under five weeks.

# 18

# THE HELL OF CANUNGRA

## MAY 1945

The following morning we were promoted to Sergeant Majors. It wasn't an impressive ceremony. As we were getting dressed a sergeant major came to the barrack where we were staying and handed Eitsick and me the brass sergeant major stripes to put on our epaulettes. As he walked out of the barrack he said without turning around 'Congratulations'. It was 24 May 1945. We were to stay at Camp Columbia until some Dutch troops came up from Casino. We were re-issued with another kitbag and a complete outfit without of course our intimate personal possessions, which in my case had not amounted to much. The troops, about twenty of them, arrived by truck at lunchtime the next day. The men got off the truck and had a lunch break. Eitsick and I were put in charge of them. After lunch we boarded the truck and went to a place called Canungra.

The Jungle Training School at Canungra was about seventy miles (about 112 kilometres) from Brisbane. Both Eitsick and I had by then already acquired jungle warfare experience, and as to the rest of the men in the platoon, all being natives of the Dutch East Indies, they had probably been born in the jungle. This Jungle Training School didn't make much sense to us but who were we to question orders from above? So to the jungle training school we went.

When we arrived there it was raining. We were taken to a sloping parade ground and made to wait. There we stood in the rain as if we had to be soaking wet before we could be admitted to this memorable institution. Although the whole set up was run by the Australian army, a Dutch sergeant major was there and he took charge of us, including Eitsick and I. We were told to take out our canteens and mess gears. An order was given that every second man in the line was to tear his blanket in half and give the other half to the man beside him. Having done all that we were told to leave our kitbags on the ground and march away into the bush. I sarcastically thought 'There goes my new kitbag.'

Eitsick, a little further down the line winked at me and I knew he also had the same thought. What can be said about the Canungra Jungle Training School? It was strenuous. It was tough. It was difficult. It was rough. It was rugged. It was demanding both morally and physically. It was a struggle no matter what you did or where you went. It was a constant

169

pressure on our mental and physical performance. It was a constant painful demand on our energy. In brief it was a ridiculous infliction of punishment on all of us who had already experienced the real thing and had found it to be far less demanding than what we were facing there now.

All we did was march day and night on compass headings with targets suddenly popping up here and there. We had to attack hills where there was no enemy to kill. We had to crawl though obstacles that we had never come across before nor any time later. We crossed creeks hanging with our hands and legs to a rope; a performance that was not likely ever to materialise in actual combat. We fed on miserable K rations when bloody good food could, at least, easily have been brought over to us. In one word it was hell. We washed our underwear in filthy slimy creek water and most of the time we slept in the bush feeding the mosquitoes, which had acquired a taste for yellowed Atabrine flesh. The concept behind this entire savage exercise must have been, 'If you survived in the islands we'll get you here.' As indeed we did have quite a few accidents. One night I was talking to the Dutch Sergeant Major in charge of us and I told him in no uncertain terms what I thought of his Jungle School. He laughed and said,

'What are you crapping about, I've been here eight months and every three weeks I go through this all over again.' After that I felt that it was uncharitable to complain. The end eventually came and we all knew that, whatever would come up next, after Canungra it would be like a holiday. And a holiday it was. From Canungra we drove to Camp Columbia and then straight to Casino. Back to the old camp. Two days later I was again on my way to Seymour. This time Eitsick and I were to attend the OCTU. The Officer Corps Training Unit. It was an institution, which catapulted sergeants and sergeant majors into an officers' mess in a matter of weeks. There we met two other Dutch boys, they were both also sergeant majors. One was called Paulus and the other De Sauvagie. They both came from Melbourne. The course was very interesting. We spent long hours at it but it was more class work than slogging around in the mud. Although we still did some of it. We were taught to command with respect. To assess how much one could reasonably expect from a man's performance both in physical and mental demands. We also learnt a few basic military tactics. How to recognise different toxic gases and a lot of other things.

One facet of every exercise was the high regard held for human life. If a certain plan of action was contemplated a reasonable casualty expectation had to be established based on different factors. We also went over a lot of studies that we had already covered at the Junior Leader School but this time in more depth. After about five weeks of that, Eitsick and I were called back to Brisbane for another field experience tour. It was the last week in July. We went directly from Seymour to Sydney by train. In those days one had to change trains at Albury. The train tracks' width in New South Wales was different from those in Victoria. We arrived in Sydney in the morning and that night we took a train to Brisbane.

We arrived there the next morning. We were picked up at the South Brisbane station and driven to Wacol. There we reported to the Dutch Headquarters at Camp Columbia and we were immediately made *Vaandrig*; Ensigns in English. We were given

171

our little silver stars. With pride we pinned one on each of our epaulettes. We were now considered to be officers, but still below the rank of second lieutenant. It was only a wartime commission. It was meticulously explained to us that if we wanted to stay in the army after the war we would still have to qualify from 'a proper officer's school'.

'After the war!' I thought. Could we possibly live that long? I was eighteen and a half years old.

Later that day the Fourth Infantry Company arrived by truck from Casino. They were all natives of the Dutch East Indies. This time Captain Lewtein put me in command of the First Infantry platoon. I was now in charge of about forty men.

# 19

# AMERICA DROPS THE BOMB

## JULY 1945

The following morning we were taken by truck from Wacol to the South Brisbane railway station again. There was a large space in front of it and we assembled there waiting for orders. We were sure that we were going to catch a train to somewhere, but we didn't. We reported to Captain Lewtein and he told us that we were going to march through Brisbane to go aboard a ship. Although we were now officers he did not then tell us what our ultimate destination was going to be.

The march was spectacular enough. The KNIL (The Netherlands East Indies Army) had a special parade step. Normal marching in the KNIL was the same step as any other army, left, left, one two three four. But the KNIL also had a

173

special parade step, in the same way as the English and Australian Armies have the Slow March for special ceremonies. The KNIL parade step was a little like the German goose step except that the leading foot hits the ground not with its heel but with the foot totally flat. We marched that way from the top of the Victoria Bridge, in front of the Treasury building, down Queen Street, all the way to Petrie Bight. Along the way, from the footpaths, people cheered and clapped. When we reached the old Customs House we resumed normal step and marched down the right lane to somewhere under the Storey Bridge. There we boarded a small Dutch troop transport. Later in the day a few Australian army and airforce men also came aboard and that night we left.

When we were out at sea Captain Lewtein told us that we were going to Darwin. Our ship was a coal burner. Three days after we left Brisbane we stopped at Bowen. Apparently in those days Bowen was a renowned coal station. We were not allowed to go ashore. We spent the day there.

That evening Captain Lewtein called us to his cabin and told us that we were going to Darwin to join an Australian detachment which was going to land in Timor. During the night we were on our way again. The next morning when we went on deck the sea was calm and the weather fine. To port, quite close really, we could see the Australian coast gently slipping by. It was 7 August 1945. At about 10am one of the ship's officers came down from the bridge and posted a news sheet on the news board. It was great news. The day before a plane of the United States Airforce had dropped an Atomic Bomb on Hiroshima in Japan. The Japanese Emperor had been given seventy-two hours to surrender unconditionally. The tumultuous reaction on board was unbelievable.

After a while of course the big question on everyone's lips was: 'What on earth is an Atomic Bomb?' Within an hour another bulletin on the board informed us that the city of Hiroshima had been completely destroyed by the bomb but there was no reply from the Japanese Emperor. As we were talking in Captain Lewtein's cabin, I recalled that just before the war two French scientists had died in an explosion which had destroyed their laboratory in Paris. It was said that they had been experimenting in the study of atoms. The destruction of a laboratory is understandable but a whole city? My recollection of that event still did not answer our question as to what an Atomic Bomb was. For the next two days the Atomic Bomb topic was ubiquitous. Then another bulletin stuck on the board told us that a second Atomic Bomb had been dropped on Nagasaki. This time it had the expected salutary effect. In principle the war was over. It took another couple of days for us to reach Darwin.

When we arrived we tied up at the end of a long wooden jetty sticking out into the harbour. We were all given passes to go into town. But it wasn't a town. It was a large military camp; no civilians, only soldiers, sailors and airmen. The place had been badly damaged by Japanese air raids. There was a strange feeling prevailing around the town. The war was over and somehow no one seemed to accept it. It had lasted too long to suddenly be over in a couple of days. In town I picked up an army issue newspaper which explained in a very basic manner the tremendous amount of energy which is released when an atom is destroyed. It gave details of Einstein's equation of energy being equal to the mass multiplied by the square of the speed of light. It also gave information regarding the effect of the bomb and the total destruction of the two cities and speculated as to the expected number of casualties. Obviously this atomic bomb business was brand new and no one knew much about it. Not even whoever he was who had written all this. Radioactivity wasn't mentioned. Of course most of the fellows I spoke to had never heard of Einstein let alone his equation. And now that they had heard of him and his equation no one still knew what the hell he was talking about anyway. Darwin didn't have much appeal. It was like walking around the camp in Casino with nothing to do. At mid-day I went back to the ship for lunch.

After that, in the cabin, we discussed the Atomic Bomb. That was all that anybody wanted to talk about. From that army newspaper we knew a little more about it but not very much. We could not understand that one bomb, only one, could destroy a city the size of Sydney. It was inconceivable. It was of a magnitude which was beyond comprehension. Just one bomb! That evening I decided to go to the pictures. I had seen a cinema in town and noted that it was still working but only at night. I walked around the main street, went into a canteen and bought a tin of sliced peaches. That was a mistake because I couldn't open it and no one had a tin opener. In desperation I managed to requisition the bayonet of an Australian soldier who was standing guard in front of a building and opened the bloody tin with it on the edge of the footpath while the soldier was laughing his head off. I 'drank' the peaches straight out of the tin and walked over to the cinema. It was run by the army.

When I walked in I realised why it only showed movies at night. It was only half a cinema. Two or three yards beyond the entrance it had no roof. A white screen at the end and some make-do seats had been arranged in the open air but the rest of the building had gone during one of the Japs' bombing raids. I forgot what the movie was but I must have enjoyed it. I only remember the bad ones. After that I walked back to the jetty with some of the boys. When we reached the wooden jetty we thought the ship had left without us. We could not see it where it had been. Then we realised that the tide had gone out and our transport was about twenty-five feet (about 7.5 metres) lower from where it had been when we left it. We stayed on the ship a few days then one night, while we were asleep, we left Darwin.

The convoy to Timor was not at all as impressive as the one to Tarakan. It was evident that those higher up in the Military scale had in fact accepted that the war was over. We on the other hand only hoped that the Japs had accepted it as well because if they had not, by the perceivable strength of the convoy, we were in for a monumental fiasco. Luckily it was not to be. The ships arrived in front of Kupang. There was a small beach there. We stopped. Landing crafts came alongside and we climbed down into them. We all took off to the beach together. When we landed it was very strange. There was a small parapet at the top end of the beach and we could see Japanese soldiers behind it. There we stood on the sand at the water's edge at the bottom of the beach looking at them and they at us. Eventually some of them began throwing their rifles over the parapet and we realised that they knew the war was over. As it turned out later, some of them didn't know or did not want to know, but for the time being it was a strange but manageable situation. As we stood there on the beach an Australian Major and a few other Australian Officers came over to us. They wanted to know if we had a Japanese interpreter with us. We didn't, we told them that we thought they had one. Captain Lewtein called me over, and also some of the other Dutch officers. After a short deliberation it was decided that we would leave the men on the beach for the time being and that we, the group of officers would go and try to contact the Japanese officers.

Some of our officers were left on the beach with the men, many of whom, by now, were getting pretty agitated. We started to walk towards a gap we could see in the parapet. Before we reached it a ranked Japanese soldier came over to us, bowed, and signaled to us to follow him. He took us to a house nearby. The captain told us to wait outside while he, and the Australian officers went in. I and two other Ensigns, Rudy Regout and Jan Den Hartog just stood there outside the house. Quite a number of Timorese civilians were going about their business unperturbed by the somewhat suspenseful atmosphere. Some came over and shook our hands; others totally ignored us.

While we were standing there a number of empty Japanese trucks arrived. At the same time all the officers including five or six Japanese officers came out of the house. One of the Japanese officers thought he could speak English but we could not understand him. The Australian Major was in charge and as he spoke we had to translate into Malay everything he said to the Japanese Officers. It was slow but in the end we managed to get it across. One of the Japs' officers said he had expected us to use the harbour and tie up at the wharf. Apparently we could have done that.

Then we passed on the order from the Australian Major that all the Japanese, including the officers, were to surrender their weapons. We made them throw their weapons on a stack on the ground. The officers surrendered their swords as well as their hand guns. Later the Japanese soldiers were made to climb aboard their trucks and they were taken away. Their officers remained there with us. They were not prisoners of war, the war was over, they were free. This unprecedented situation, with all its potentially disastrous eventualities was discussed with them. It was then decided, in order to avoid any unpleasant confrontations between their soldiers and ours, that the Japanese soldiers should be taken to their camps and that they should remain there until they could be repatriated to Japan. Of course we had no idea when that would be possible. The Japanese officers of course were given, within reason and not to be abused, free rein of the place. Later that day we heard some rifle shots in the distance. It did not last long. Some Japs had obviously decided to take a last shot at the enemy. The way we ourselves felt we could quite understand their motivation. These occurrences, unfortunately, went on for quite a number of days after we landed in Timor.

The Australian troops established their camp not far on the other side of the town. It was a nice spot close to a beach and the sea. We marched a few miles inland to a place which had been suggested by one of the Japanese Officers. It had been a Japanese camp and we, the officers at least, had thatched bamboo huts to sleep in. That night for dinner we were back on the Netherlands

East Indies Army's famous battle rations: boiled rice and a tin of sardines. That remained the standard menu for the Dutch troops for well over a month. We managed to get ourselves some K rations but after a few days of that I was glad to go back to the rice and sardines. Sometimes the natives would bring *kerbao* (buffalo) stew in big jar-like containers made of cut trunk pieces of bamboo. We could buy these or exchange them for cigarettes. Most of the Dutch boys wouldn't touch them. It was too spicy for them. I didn't mind; in fact I liked it. It was as close to home cooking as one could get and it certainly was a lot better than tinned sardines. Besides after my first meal at Camp Columbia nothing was ever too spicy for me again.

The day after our arrival in Timor we received a full fleet of trucks and jeeps and ducks. It seemed to have been initially overlooked that after landing we would have required transport. Now we were mobile again. We established our motor pool and Rudy Regout was put in charge of it. It was located at the aerodrome, which was the most suitable place for it to be. There were a couple of sheds there and the few airforce mechanics refuelling the planes could easily attend to the trucks and the jeeps if they had to.

One afternoon we were told to assemble at the aerodrome. The official Japanese surrender was to take place there. Pretty well on time, a Japanese plane with big white patches painted on the fuselage and on the wings made its approach to the aerodrome. It landed safely but half way down the gravel runway it blew a tyre, veered to port, and crashed in the forest which lined the strip. They were all killed. Another plane came in a week or so later to sign the surrender but I wasn't there then. Now the war was over. Life in post war occupation was rather simple. Basically we had nothing to do. From time to time we would drive to a Japanese compound with a jeep and a truck and we would collect their weapons. Their officers would supervise the loading of the weapons and swords into our truck and we would take them back to one of the huts in our camp. I secured for myself a Japanese Officer's sword and a hand gun as souvenirs. Actually all of us did.

On other occasions we would board an LST and go to other islands to collect Japanese soldiers who had been left there. We went to Sumba, to Sumbawa, to Flores and even once as far as Bali. On most of these islands the Japs had already been picked up either by the Australians or by the Americans. I did enjoy these trips. It was interesting to discover the different lifestyles and customs between one island and another. They were the same people with the same culture and background yet their existence was always somewhat different. One day, straight after lunch, we were called on parade. The entire company had to line up for an official inspection.

We officers, on such occasions had to wear our Klewang, a Dutch East Indies Army's issue sword. It was about three feet long and slightly curved. As the troops were ordered to 'present arms', we had to draw swords and hold them up vertically with the pommel in front of our face. That day's special parade was an inspection of the Australian and Dutch contingent by Marshall Blamey. As he walked along the ranks in the company of other Australian officers and our Dutch company commander, Captain Lewtein, we had to draw sword and stand at attention.

The ceremonial drawing of the sword demanded a fair amount of space in front. Because I was in command of the first platoon, my men were the first to stand inspection. Marshall Blamey and his entourage came close to the ranks to start the inspection and at that point I had to salute with my sword. There wasn't enough room for the drill. Blamey probably thought that I was going to chop his head off and jumped back a few feet. The men started to laugh and in the end we all did, as well as Marshall Blamey himself.

One evening, as it was getting dark, I heard a big commotion in the camp. I was officer of the week and it was my duty to see what this was all about. When I got there the soldiers were lynching a young Japanese soldier. He was only a kid. I had to fire two shots of my gun in the air before I got any attention. One of the soldiers brought me a Japanese hand grenade. He told me that the Jap had crawled between the tents and had thrown the grenade in one of them. Luckily it had not exploded. By then the poor bastard was unconscious on the ground. I took the hand grenade and told two men to take the Japanese soldier to the Military Police compound.

This was the sort of event that we had been warned about. I defused the grenade and emptied the powder out of it. I kept it as a souvenir. I think my son Malcom has it. We were often informed by the natives that pockets of Japanese soldiers were still pushing the natives around in some of the *kampongs*. We would send a patrol to investigate but usually the Japs would have gone. It actually got to the stage where we did not pay attention anymore to that sort of gossip. Many of these indeed related to events which had occurred while the war was still on.

# 20

# A MACHINE TO MAKE MONEY

## AUGUST 1945

A few weeks after we had settled in Timor we received news that a company of Japanese infantry was still in charge in a town near the Portuguese border. The place was called Atambua. I was detailed to go there with my platoon and take their surrender. I had no idea how far it was from Kupang. Our army map of Timor only showed in detail the coast line and a few miles inland. The rest was all blank. Terra incognita. The villages, called *kampongs*, were clearly marked on the map along the coast, so were the creeks and the rivers but they disappeared just a short distance inland. I had no idea where Atambua was. It was marked as a dot on the blank portion of my map but gave no indication as to how to get there nor how far it was. I made inquiries from some of the local civilians who claimed to have been there. The next day, with two of them to guide us, we were on our way. We went with two trucks. About forty of us plus the two guides. According to them there was a good road going there. We hadn't gone very far before I realised that these two jokers didn't have much of a clue as to where Atambua was. Every time we passed a *kampong* they would ask us to stop and they would get information from the villagers.

By then I didn't care much. I knew we had to go east and as long as the road led us eastwards I knew that sooner or later in one of the *kampong*s some one would have heard of Atambua and would know how to get there. Another thing I discovered on that trip was that the natives had no idea of what a kilometre was. The Malay word for kilometre is kilo. *Dari disini ke Atambua berapa kilo?* (From here to Atambua how many kilometres?) The answer would vary according to whether you were on foot or in a jeep or a truck. If you were on foot the answer would be: *Baniak, baniak kilo tuan, telaloo baniak.* (Much, much kilometres, Sir, too much). If you were in a Jeep the answer would be: *Sedikit, juma sedikit kilo tuan.* (Little, only little kilometres, Sir). It was obvious that to them kilometre would mean, not the distance, but the time it would take to get there with the facility at hand.

I am quite confident that by now, after sixty years, they finally got it right. Before the war, the road to Atambua must have been the main road along the length of the Island. When we got there it was dirt but it was a reasonable road. Reasonable except that the Japanese, during the occupation of the Island, had not seen it as important to maintain it in reasonable condition. So the road to Atambua, where it weathered the bad conditions, was still reasonably good, but where it did not, it was washed out, guttered or even in places it was totally gone. So to us, Atambua, even though we were in trucks, instead of being 'Little, very little' turned out to be '*Baniak, baniak*'. Much much. We didn't get there until the next day although it was only a little over two hundred kilometres away. When we arrived we drove to the Japanese garrison. I left the men in the trucks and walked into the Japanese compound with a couple of my sergeants. We were met by a number of Japanese officers, a couple of them spoke reasonably good English. They told me that they knew we were coming and had decided to stay there until we arrived to keep things under control.

Late that afternoon they vacated the compound and my men occupied it. It was a great set up. Before the war Atambua had obviously been an important town close to the Portuguese border. The compound had been a solid military installation made of brick and mortar buildings with tile roofs, running water and all proper military facilities. In fact it was a lot better than what we had at Kupang. Nearby was a street with a number of brick villas which, pre-war, had been occupied by Dutch officers and their families. A Chinese doctor now lived in one of them with his wife and a few kids and I settled myself down in a villa next to him. The town had not been damaged by the war. There were the usual variety of shops and public buildings employing the usual variety of public servants.

One of the first things I did was to call on the local equivalent of the town Mayor, the *kapala kampong*, to acquaint myself with some of the most urgent civic problems. The answer was

185

quite specific and straight to the point. Money!. When I arrived in Atambua, although the war had been over for nearly two months, I discovered that the civilian population was still using Japanese printed guilders. These had replaced the Royal Dutch Guilders during the Japanese Occupation. They were very basic pieces of paper printed on both sides with the words 'Japanese Empire' and the amount of guilders as to their value. Different amount notes were printed in different colours. Since the end of the war the local population was reluctant to accept these Guilders as legal tender but since there was as yet no alternative they did not have any choice. The Japanese Empire Guilders did however suffer a humiliating deflationary demise. In the local markets its value was now one tenth of what it had been during the Japanese Occupation. The day after we arrived the Japanese garrison left Atambua for Kupang. They went unescorted in a large convoy of trucks and light jeep like vehicles. A tremendous amount of Japanese material was left behind, unfortunately petrol was not part of it.

One day as I was looking around the Military Police compound I unlocked one of the cells. There, in front of me, to my great surprise was the sublime dream of every young man. A machine to print money. Japanese money alas! But money just the same. It was not the sophisticated type of note printing machine one sees on television in documentaries of the Royal Mint. It was a very simple device, which would print only one note at a time. Although the plates could be changed to accommodate higher denominations this one was fitted with a pair of half Guilder plates and there were no other plates to be seen anywhere. On a table nearby and on the floor were stacks of precut sheets of paper ready to be printed. Looking at all of this I couldn't help smiling and thinking of the *dolce vita* those Japs must have enjoyed during the three-year Occupation of the island. It took me a few days to list my most urgent needs and they obviously included more than the usual military requirements. I was there with forty soldiers to replace the entire Japanese garrison. It immediately became quite clear that my duty there now was well beyond mere military protection. Being the only Dutch representative authority in town, what was expected of me by the local people and public servants, was more than what I had been sent to Atambua for. It quickly became apparent that my duties there also included the re-establishment of the prewar Dutch civil system. This of course had not been included in my military training. Luckily in my new endeavour I was superbly assisted by the local dignitaries. They all magnificently rose to the occasion. All I had to do was to agree with what they were proposing and supply the money to do it with. It worked out extremely well.

I contacted Kupang and explained my predicament. I was told to cooperate fully with the local civil authorities until further development. Since this was exactly what I had been doing up till then I was quite relieved. The next day three jeeps arrived from Kupang. They were bringing money. Big canvas bags full of coins. No notes. Since the miserable decline in the value of the Japanese printed Guilders, the local natives had totally lost faith in paper money. By now they only wanted the silver or bronze coins. To their satisfaction the silver Royal Dutch Guilder was now once again in circulation. From time to time we would get information about small groups of Japanese soldiers still living in various out of the way *kampongs*. Worse than this were reports of raids made by Portuguese Timorese tribes on Dutch side *kampongs*. The East side of Timor had been colonized by Portugal in the mid-sixteenth century. In 1767 the Dutch began to colonize the Western portion of the island. The confrontation between the two governments eventually led to the Treaty of Lisbon in 1859 when the island was formally divided in two parts. Knowing that the Japanese had been defeated, the Portuguese natives who raided the Dutch side *kampongs* relied on the territorial protection provided by the now supposedly reinstated international border between the two halves of Timor.

To be quite honest the Dutch side natives probably also put their faith on the same border to prevent Portuguese army patrols from pursuing them after they had raided Portuguese side *kampongs*. The natives on both sides of the border were extremely savage and aggressive. These raids were without mercy, from either side. They would raid a *kampong*, kill as many of the inhabitants as stood in their way, steal their livestock and supplies and retreat beyond the border where they could not be pursued by the authorities of the offended side. In some of these raided *kampongs* I have seen dead women lying flat on the ground, naked from the waist down, with corn cobs stuck in their vagina. With a contingent of only forty odd men I was hardly in a position to attempt any policing of the border area. This had to wait until more military support came up.

This military support came two or three weeks later. A further two platoons and a Command Group under the command of a Dutch officer called Murling. We were now a full military strength Company, stationed in Atambua. Captain Murling was an ex KNIL Air Force officer. He had been transferred to the Dutch peacetime occupation army probably for his administrative skills. He was a tall slim sort of a man in his mid twenties with an enthusiastic and engaging personality. I had never met him before but I liked him straight away. I admired his competence and we soon became friends. Within a few days he managed to contact whoever was in charge of the Portuguese forces on the other side of the border in order to put an end to the vicious raids which had escalated since the end of the war. Since most of the natives on both sides of the border were equally guilty we soon came to a manageable agreement with the Portuguese. If a *kampong* was being raided and we could manage to get there in time or soon after we would contact the Portuguese as soon as possible and pursue the raiders irrespective of the border, until they were in a position to take over from us. The arrangement was reciprocal. In total disregard of the border, the Portuguese would pursue and arrest any of the Dutch natives who had raided *kampongs* on the Portuguese side until we could take over from them. Although this was a somewhat rhetorical agreement it seemed to achieve, up to a point, the desired effect. Reports of *kampongs* being raided became less frequent.

I, with my platoon, was assigned the task of constantly patrolling the southern section of the border area where many of these raids were taking place. The area was very wild with lots of mountains and deep valleys. The task was very physically demanding. We were either in thick steaming jungle sharing the area with millions of mosquitoes and all other vermin which enjoy that sort of atmosphere or we were up a five or six thousand foot mountain top grassland in beautiful fresh air that the jungle refused to invade. Of course up there, even though the grass was greener and the air was purer, thirst persisted and water was a lot harder to find. In all the time that this patrolling went on we never managed to pursue, let alone catch any of the offenders. Whenever we reached a *kampong* which had been raided we were always too late. The raiders had already left leaving behind only carnage and destruction. Nevertheless, probably due to our constant presence on our side of the border and the Portuguese equivalent on the other side, these vicious raids finally came to an end. One day in one of these patrols, marching at compass heading, we came across a large extent of very swampy land. It was somewhere near the southern coast of the Island. We were still in the blank area of the map. The land was without striking features and the height of the reeds in the marshes prevented any visual orientation. After several attempts to find a way around it I decided to march on through it on our initial heading. The water was only about a foot deep but we had to chop our way through the reeds. After about ten hours of excruciating labour we had to call it a day. Going back by then was out of the question.

We had to settle as best we could, where we were. Cutting reeds and stacking them down into the water we made a number of small platforms high enough to lay down on, and be out of the water. Dinner that night was cold boiled rice, which we carried for such emergencies and the reliable tins of sardines. The rice was cooked before we left in small pillow type containers made of woven palm tree leaves. The little woven pillows would be half filled with rice, closed and tossed into boiling water. When cooked the rice would expand and fill the little pillows. It was ingenious and easy to carry. It could fit in a pocket. I don't think any of us slept that night. I for one could feel the stack of reeds gradually compressing down into the water. Mosquitoes and leeches were our biggest problem. We were all wearing puttees between our shoes and our trousers but each of us had at least half a dozen leeches stuck to our calves. How they ever got there no one knew. The way to get rid of them was to burn them off with a cigarette. For mosquitoes we carried four-gallon cans of kerosene. We rubbed it on our arms and faces like we would do today with Aerogard or such other modern mosquito repellant. The next day was much of the same except that one of my men had a leech, which had partially crawled inside his penis. He tried to pull it out but of course he only got half of it off. The head stayed inside. Unable to pass water except in odd drops, the poor devil was in excruciating pain. We couldn't leave him there and we could not carry him either so he had to walk. We tried everything to no avail to get that leech out. In the end I filled a tin with kerosene and told him to hold it and walk with his penis soaking in it. It was a great laugh for all the rest of the platoon but I am sure the poor devil did not share our sense of humour. That day I decided to stop earlier so that we could settle ourselves down more comfortably. The water was a little deeper but there were plenty of reeds and that night, using some of the kerosene in a tin, we managed to boil some water and make some tea. That night also, with a great scream of relief, our friend with the leech managed to pass water and successfully eject the other half of that little miserable squatter which had taken residence inside his penis. To his great amazement the entire platoon clapped and cheered the event. After 'de-leeching' ourselves as best we could we settled down for the night.

I couldn't sleep. I was concerned by the fact that we had gone two days through this damned swamp and had no idea where it would end. If the water got too deep we would have to turn back. Turn back how far? I had no idea how far we had gone. The chopping down of reeds of course had slowed us a lot. In relation to actual distance we certainly had not gone very far but it had taken us two days. Should I decide to go back or should we keep going? In the morning I decided to go on. As we got going the water in places became less deep and we all thought that we were nearly out of it. By late afternoon we had averaged a greater distance that we had in each of the previous days but there was still no sign of dry land. I decided once again to stop early for the night. The men started to cut reeds and stack them.

Suddenly a great yell from a short distance interrupted the monotonous whingeing of the men. One man had wandered away to do something very private when he stumbled onto dry land. We all dropped everything and got ourselves out of the swamp. We were so tired that most of us collapsed as we reached dry land. I fell asleep on my face with my feet still in the water, leeches and all. It wasn't until the early hours of the morning that I managed to crawl right out of that bog.

The next day I declared a day of rest. We all deserved it. I took a few bearings and roughly entered on the blank portion of my military map the approximate position of the swamp. It was a hope and guess type of entry. I could only enter a straight line, the direction that we had sloughed through that quagmire. As to distance covered, it was pure guess. And of course I was in no position to estimate its width either. For all I knew, without any field of sight, we might have been marching three days in a straight line in the middle of a watercourse. During the afternoon I felt a fit of malaria coming on. I didn't get it often but sometimes I did. Headache and fever and shakes. I kind of put up with it until night time. By then it was getting worse. Luckily I had developed a quick, even if somewhat unorthodox, cure for it. I would swallow four or five quinine tablets and drink a full glass of *sopy*. I would then lay down, cover myself and shake until my teeth nearly fell out. Then I would pass out and wake up four or five hours later bright as a button. It worked every time and it did that night also. Sopy was a great standby. It was an alcohol made by fermenting coconut milk. It wasn't an army issued ration but every man had his own little supply. We shut our eyes to it; for like the splicing of the main brace with rum in the navy; at times it had its benefits. Of course we always tried to give to it a flavour or a taste which it was never intended to have. We were always trying to transform this methylated spirit tasting brew into something more palatable, like whisky perhaps. With shoe polish we had managed to give it the required colour, but no matter what other additive we tried, the taste always came out disgustingly disappointing. We tried all sorts of things, from crushed betel nuts, or that herb that they make mosquito coils with, to the actual sex parts of male crocodiles. Apparently, according to the natives, that last one imparted to *sopy* a certain degree of aphrodisiac property. Personally all I wanted out of it was that it should taste somewhere like whisky but alas it never did.

One morning as we were patrolling some of the blank area of my army map we heard the sound of a bell. I didn't know which day it was but it could have been a Sunday. We were all surprised. I had no idea where we were and the clear sound of a bell way out in the jungle was a strange feeling. I decided to head towards it. Within minutes we heard the laughs and screams of children playing. Then shortly after, we stumbled on to it. In the middle of a grass clearing stood a beautiful little white church. It looked every bit like the churches we have in Australia and those in Europe except for its size. It was very small, built of bricks and painted white. Not far from it were a number of other buildings also painted white.

As we entered the clearing a priest came out of the church and stood there. He was wearing a white cassock and waving at us. We stopped; I walked over to him and we introduced ourselves. He was a Catholic bishop. The place was a Mission called Lahurus. It wasn't on the map. It was called Lahurus because of the mountain on which it stood. There were also a number of Dutch nuns; all dressed in white and the Bishop introduced me to them. After a short conversation and an invitation to lunch the bishop excused himself.

It was indeed Sunday and the ringing of the bell had been to call the parishioners to mass. I, in an expected act of devotion to good public relations, dragged my agnostic carcass into the church and attended mass with all the others. After mass I joined the bishop in his quarters. We had a few drinks while waiting for lunch. Apparently the bishop had found a far more palatable way of doctoring *sopy* than we had. During the meal even some of it almost tasted like wine. I, several times, congratulated him for his chemistry skills on *sopy* but no matter how many times I vaunted his ability and expressed my interest he never divulged his secrets. So for us it still had to be crushed betel nuts and crocodile pricks. Lunch was a feast out of this world. A meal fit for kings. It had been prepared and served at our table by the nuns. They ate somewhere else. I thoroughly enjoyed this gastronomic feast which I thought now had just become a thing of the past. My men also managed to cook a good lunch with some added meat supplied by the nuns. After our meal, during coffee, a lot of shouting could be heard outside. The bishop said apologetically that it wasn't serious, 'Cock fights' he said. He explained that the duty of the church was to bring in new light without destroying too many local customs.

When I walked out I saw what the commotion was all about. I walked over to a large group of men shouting and gesticulating around a small arena about ten feet (about 3 metres) in diameter. In the centre two men were showing off their prize fighting cocks. Each of the birds had a vicious looking curved knife strapped to one leg. Coins were changing hands amongst the crowd. Then the two men lowered their birds to the ground and let them go. The two cocks immediately got stuck into each other and in less than one minute one of them was out of action. As I walked away in disgust the crowd was cheering and placing bets once more for the next event. That afternoon we left Lahurus, trekked south for a few hours and made camp.

# 21

# THE BORDER
# BETWEEN EAST AND
# WEST TIMOR

## 1946

By then we were well into 1946. The second war to end all wars had been fought and won. So what was there for us to do now? Playing soldiers for the rest of our lives like kids play cowboys and Indians? That wasn't for me. So the next time that I was in Atambua I asked Murling.

'How long is this going to go on for?'

I knew his answer before he told me. 'I have no idea.'

That night I wrote a letter to the KNIL Headquarters in Batavia requesting to be discharged from the army so that I could resume my interrupted studies. I never got a reply. The border between Dutch and Portuguese Timor we all knew existed. We all, on both sides, by now had a fair idea where it was or where it was supposed to be. There was, however, no borderline or fence or marks where it exactly was. Generations ago, apparently, a few cairns had been erected in secluded places and very far apart. Some of them could still possibly be found but most of them, we were told, had completely ceased to exist. So one day, just back from patrol, I was called to Captain Murling's Office. There were two other officers there. One I knew; it was Jerry Lemmens. The other I had never seen before. Murling had a few theodolites on his desk. He asked Jerry and me if we knew how to use them. We both said no. Apparently the other chap there was an expert and during the afternoon he taught Jerry and I how to use the gadgets. Actually it wasn't very different from the directional compass that we had been using all this time. It just indicated vertical angles as well as direction. Jerry and I were not particularly impressed with the thing but the man made such an issue of it that we both feigned a deep interest in what he said and left it at that.

Of course we did not suspect it at the time but the idea behind this exercise was to re-survey the border. The next day we were acquainted with it. The 'expert' was given the northern section of it, Jerry the middle part east of the Lahurus mountain and I the southern end to the Timor sea. Our instructions were to try to find the old cairns and or make new marks where there were none. We were given a list of headings and distances which were noted on a map. We were not to erect the cairns but simply to erect some kind of reference where they should be. The cairns were to be built later by 'others'. Thank God for that. I couldn't see us carrying all our gear and lugging a few bags of cement as well as ballast. That was definitely a job for civilian employees. The next day at first light, we were ready to leave. Our last instruction from Captain Murling had been to be 'practical'. When I asked what he meant by that he had replied: 'Be practical… you know what I mean… a few metres one side or the other are not going to make much difference.' So I left. With my platoon we headed south-east. I had to find a *kampong* called Besikama. That was a village close to the Timor Sea and supposedly close to where the border was expected to be. We walked all day. We had a couple of rest breaks but we did not have lunch. The terrain at first was difficult, lots of mountains.

Later, as we were getting close to the coast, it gradually became more amenable. Later still we finally reached walking tracks with footprints on them. We were getting close to somewhere. On a clear stretch of the track we came across a woman coming the other way. She was carrying a large flat basket on her head. We could smell its contents as she approached. It smelled like our own fish and chips. Having gone all day without food the men asked her if she wanted to sell some of it. She nodded, brought down the basket, took off a cloth which was covering the food and we all licked our lips. Lovely roasted mackerel looking chunks, still hot and juicy.

We all purchased some and thoroughly enjoyed the little savouries. The woman could speak Malay so I asked her in Malay what the name of that fish was and she said, '*Itu tidah Ikant, tuan, itu ular'*.' This is not fish, Sir, it is snake.' I was so surprised that I bought another piece and ate it.

In Timor, Malay was the official language but the Timorese had their own tongue. Quite different from Malay. Many of them, especially in the *kampongs*, only spoke Timorese. I asked the woman if she knew where Besikama was and she told me she knew, she said she came from there.

'How far?'

'Only a little bit far' she said. That night we camped in the *kampong* called Besikama. The next morning I had a talk with the *kapala kampong*. The local chief. He spoke no Malay but through an interpreter he told me that the border wasn't very far. How would I find it I asked and his reply was: 'It's easy, you walk and all of a sudden you're on the other side of it. Sometimes you are this side and sometimes you are on the other side, very easy' Of course it meant nothing to me. I was hoping that he knew where at least one of the cairns was but the old man didn't know what I was talking about. Later that day we walked to the sea and headed north east. The map I had, with the different headings and distances, was all very well but where the border started on the Timor Sea shore was not marked on it. I needed a starting point. I had none. Somewhere, I am sure, there must have been in existence a document with the starting point of the border on the southern coast of Timor entered in celestial figures; latitude and longitude. But I did not have it. Had I had it I still could not have found the spot for although I knew how to find a celestial position, I did not have a sextant to do it with.

The entire exercise had obviously been planned on the basis that some kind of vestige was still there whence we could start from. So we started to look. And look we did. For several days. We even looked inland from the coast for some kind of vestige in order to make a start but we could not find any.

I spoke to several natives that we came across, most had no idea what I was talking about. Others knew that there had been a border but had no idea where it had been. Those who supposedly knew where it was pointed sometimes ahead of us while others pointed behind. It was most frustrating. And these were local people, people who knew or should have known whether they were Dutch or Portuguese. In the end, remembering the advice to be 'practical' given to me by Captain Murling before we left, I started to look for some kind of natural prominence along the sea front where a border could logically begin. Unfortunately I was unable to find a notable river or creek or freshet that would do. Not even a drain or a runnel or a rivulet. Nothing. In the end I had to decide where the border was to be. I settled on a small promontory at the end of a very small beach. We started from there and proceeded northwards.

We followed the list of headings and the distances in between which had been given to me before we left Atambua. It was easy enough. I used my compass, never at any time did I use the theodolite, I had no reason to. And I even began to think that the 'expert' they had sent to Atambua to survey the border was not quite up to his mark. The entire width of the island in this particular area is only about eighty kilometres. My portion of it was only thirty kilometres or so. Not a very long distance. Going uphill and downhill on the various headings we might have had to cover somewhat more terrain but not that much more. The various headings, which I had been given in Atambua, all being within a few degrees of each other, practically amounted to a straight line going northwards. They did not, however, seem to coincide with any prominent features of the land.

That did not stop me from sleeping at night. I had been told to be practical and I was. Boy! Was I practical. It was also quite apparent that whoever had first pegged the original border between Dutch and Portuguese Timor had been by far more 'practical' than any of us could ever possibly be. I never found any of the original cairns. Jerry who was surveying the central section had apparently seen some stacks of stones, which he thought might have been the original pegs. But Jerry was well known for his prolific imagination so I did not pay much attention to that.

The distances which we had been given were of course supposed to be on a map. That is on a piece of paper that one can lay flat down on a table. We were tramping up mountains and down crevices and ravines. We covered a lot of distance but I had no idea how far that would have been on a flat map. In order to be able to do that we should have had a sextant, time-piece, sight reduction tables and charts; none of which we had. I could only guess the horizontal distances we covered so there again I was being 'practical'. Now and then we would collect a few rocks together to mark where we had been so that 'the others' later could erect some kind of suitable permanent effigy.

And so on we went, hoping for the best. I kept my fingers crossed and relied heavily on my 'practical' skills. Miraculously enough, after a couple of months of surveying, one good day we stumbled on Jerry Lemmens and his platoon coming south. He also had been using all his 'practical' talents to the hilt. During those months we had had a few two-day R and R in Atambua.

We went back there to get fresh supplies and the breaks were always welcome. We even picked up a bit of the local dialect, which at times came in very handy. As I remember that during one of our R and R breaks in Atambua Jerry had mentioned that 'his border' was basically a straight south-eastern line which in fact seemed to coincide with my north-western one. However now when I look at a map of Timor I see that there is a huge big bulge protruding into Portuguese territory right in the middle of the island and a small isolated pocket of it way west into what is now Indonesia. It is quite apparent that the border upon which so much of our youthful energy and perspiration was expended has since been redesigned and resurveyed. So when I look at it now I no longer feel guilty for having, at the time, so heavily indulged in my 'practical' prowess.

# 22

# BATAVIA IN JAVA

## 1946

The second half of 1946 was coming to an end. One evening, returning to Atambua after a few days patrol to Atapupu on the North Coast of the island, Murling, who by then lived next door to me, called me over for a drink. Whisky was now obtainable from the Chinese traders. As he poured me one he told me that I was being discharged to pursue my studies. Apparently my letter, which I had long since forgotten, had taken effect. Because of the unrest caused by the rising Indonesian independence movement, the Netherlands East Indies Army was not being demobilised. My discharge was somewhat special. Even Murling, thinking that I might have been some kind of scientist, wanted to know what sort of special studies it was I meant to pursue. When I told him that I had no idea and that by way of studies all I had was my senior pass we both had a good laugh and another whisky. I was being discharged; all I had to do now was to find a way of going back home. There were no troop transports that we were aware of going back to Europe and certainly nothing from Timor. We talked about it for a while and then Murling said, 'There is no hurry, get your gear together and go to Kupang, you might hitch a flight to Java from there. You'll stand a better chance of getting on a ship going to Europe if you can get to Java.' A few days later I said goodbye to Murling and all my friends. I loaded all my possessions in a jeep, and left for Kupang. There I reported to Captain Lewtein who was now in full command of the Dutch part of the island. He knew of my discharge and like Murling, advised me that my best bet was to try to get to Java. There were no scheduled transports between Timor and Java. My only chance would be to try to get a lift on a supply plane going there.

Supply planes would often land at Kupang aerodrome on their way to the islands; the problem was to get one going to Java. Having obtained all the necessary documents from Captain Lewtein I decided to take all my gear to the aerodrome and stay there until the right plane turned up. My friend Ruddy Regout, who was in charge of the motor pool, was also in charge of the aerodrome. In fact, as I mentioned before, the motor pool was situated at the aerodrome. Ruddy found me a hut where I could sleep and I settled down. There were quite a lot of planes dropping in but they all seemed to be going everywhere except Java. Many were going to Australia but that was no good to me. I was to be discharged in Holland and from Australia to go to Holland even if I could have found a ship going there it would have been with a private shipping company and I would have had to pay for my passage. So it was Java or nothing. The days were long and monotonous. I had nothing to do. Every time a plane landed and taxied in I would ask the pilot where he was going and the answer never seemed to be the one I wanted. I would stick around the aerodrome until dark then I would take a jeep and go to down town Kupang to the army cinema or to have a few drinks and a chat with some of my old mates. The aerodrome strip had no lights so there was no chance of any plane coming in at night. In fact the strip was just that, just a dirt, gravel strip, not even level. No control tower, no radio communication, just a strip and a few forty-four gallon drums of fuel for those who needed some, stacked up in front of the huts.

Just before lunch time one day, however, a B25 transport landed and taxied in for fuel. As the two pilots came out I asked one of them where they were going to. He said 'Batavia'. I knew that was in Java. In fact Batavia was the capital of the Dutch East Indies. It has since been renamed Jakarta and is now the capital of Indonesia. When I asked for a lift he said 'Have a look inside, if you think that you can find a place somewhere for yourself and your bags you're welcome.' The plane was chock–a–block with aeroplane tyres but I knew by then that I would find a place in there no matter what, even if I had to curl myself up inside one of the tyres. Straight after lunch we took off and I was on my way to Java. We landed there a little after 5pm. I reported to the local army authority at the airport and showed my documents. The man was a lieutenant and by the look on his face was as confused as I was as to where I was supposed to go to spend the night. In the end he suggested that I take a jeep and go to the Tenth Battalion garrison and talk to someone there. I had never been to Batavia; I had no idea where the Tenth Battalion garrison was. I asked him to get someone to drive me there. He did and we went.

The Tenth Battalion compound was a huge agglomeration of large brick barracks. To my amazement the compound was full of women and children running all over the place. The barracks were occupied by the now freed prisoners of war. Dutch East Indies native soldiers. Their wives and kids lived there with them. I asked the driver to take me to the Head Office and he didn't know what I was talking about. Apparently there was no Head Office at the Tenth Battalion garrison anymore.

I was about to decide to go back to the airport when I saw a native sergeant. I asked him where the army Head Quarters were and he told me that it was in the city but that there would be no one there at this time of the night. He pointed to a barrack where some officers and white sergeants sometimes stayed. 'You can try there', he said. We drove to that barrack and I went in. There was no one there. Against the walls were a lot of folding canvas beds and by the look of it some of them were being used. I found one at the end of the barrack against the end wall, which seemed unoccupied and tossed my bag on it. I then went out to the jeep but it had gone. It was too late for a feed there so I went out into town.

The main street had a *kali* running right in the middle of it. A dirty foul smelling creek with a roadway on each side and a few stone bridges here and there to get from one side to the other. It was about 8pm but the place was alive with people coming and going everywhere. Along the footpaths, next to each other, were all sorts of shops and dining places. All lit up and inviting. I walked up and down a couple of times and finally had a feed of *sate bili* from a street vendor crouched behind his portable barbecue grill. Sates are small brochettes of meat skewered on thin sticks made of split bamboo. One could have *sate ayam* (chicken), *sate bili* (pork) or *sate kambing* (mutton or most probably goat). The man would cook it for you there and then on a small portable grill and serve it dipped in very spicy *katchang* sauce. A kind of liquid peanut butter mixed with coconut and hot chillies. Once you have acquired a taste for sates it is hard to walk past one of those stands without buying at least one. I did enjoy the evening in the capital. It was a change to see all this activity.

During my walk I had a bottle of Coca-Cola that I normally wouldn't touch, but that in the circumstances I considered it to be the safest way to quench my thirst. By midnight I was back in the barrack. This time there were about a dozen chaps in it. I introduced myself and within minutes I became aware that all of us there were waiting to go back to Holland to be discharged from the army. I was the last one in the queue. Apparently there were some troop transports coming from Holland bringing fresh soldiers to face the native uprising against the Dutch. But these ships went back loaded with white Dutch families who had been interned in Japanese prison camps during the war. They, of course, had priority. The next day I went over to the Army Headquarters in the city to let them know that I was there. They weren't particularly impressed. 'There are no transports to Holland' was the emphatic answer. The dismissive way in which it was said did not generate the slightest urge to inquire further. I went back to the barrack deeply disappointed. I wished then that I had never sent that letter requesting to be discharged. At least in Timor I had my own place and a *babou* to keep it clean and cook and wash and iron my uniforms whereas here in Java all I had was a canvas bed to lay on and nothing else. I could queue up with the native soldiers and their wives and their kids to have a feed but that was all that went with it.

After a couple of days I only used the barrack to sleep in. I had nothing to do. I would go into town in the morning and just walk around all day. Eventually I did discover a few eating places where I could have a good safe meal. Later of course I discovered that meals in all those eating places were quite safe. Although my first impression of Batavia had been somewhat repulsive I later discovered that Javanese people are very clean and that these dilapidated looking eating places actually served excellent, very cleanly prepared meals.

One morning as I was walking around discovering the city, I came across an old friend of mine, Willy Hogerslag. He had been transferred from Hollandia to Borneo and then to Java. He congratulated me on my promotion. He was still a sergeant major and was now attached to some army motor pool in Batavia. We had lunch together and he told me about the road convoys to Bandong. Apparently the Indonesian freedom movement was quite active in Java. The Japanese, in order to keep uprisings to a minimum during the occupation, had promised the Javanese their full independence at the end of the war. Now of course that promise was somewhat diluted by the

Japanese defeat and the Javanese were not going to take no for an answer.

Willy was telling me that although Batavia itself was more or less secured, out of town the Pelopors were quite active. The road supply convoys to Bandong were often attacked by these Javanese freedom fighters. Old Sukarno was already stirring up the insurrection and he had quite a following. They had their own camps, a lot of weapons taken from the Japs and adequate means of transport. They had adopted the red and white banner as their new Indonesian flag and their war cry was: '*Merdeka tidah djadi*'. Freedom has not come yet. After lunch Willy offered to show me his set up at the motor pool. We got into his jeep and we were on our way. On his way there he decided to show me some of the nice spots near Batavia. We drove around to different places admiring the beautiful, luscious green vegetation. Some unbelievably clear water creeks, entirely concealed under immense over-hanging trees, looked like the centre aisle of some majestic cathedral. Singing birds instead of organ music. Willy and I left the jeep and walked around for a while. It was such a relief from the hustle and bustle of the stinking city.

We sat down and talked about what was ahead of us now that the war was over. Willy had served two five-year stretches in the French Foreign Legion in North Africa. He had deserted the Legion during his third stretch when the French Vichy government had ordered the Legionnaires to fight the Americans who had landed in Morocco. Many Legionnaires who had no time for Petain and his collaborating clique had done the same. That is why he was stationed in the English

Army camp in Algiers way back when I first met him in forty-four. Since then our paths had often crossed. We had both gone to England on the same ship. We met again in Wolverhampton and later Brisbane and the last time had been in Hollandia in New Guinea. He was a good mate and we always got on well together. He was like a father to me, always coming up with what I should do and not do.

That afternoon he wanted to know what sort of studies I was being discharged for, to pursue. I told him I had no idea. His future was even more uncertain. He had no family and had spent all his life in the army, in Holland first, then in the French Foreign Legion and now in the Dutch East Indies Army. He had absolutely no idea how he would perform as a civilian. He told me that much and I felt sorry for him. We had a couple of smokes and then we went back to the jeep and got going. He kept driving around turning left here, right there, and right again and again and after a while I jokingly asked him if he knew where he was going. In a burst of laughter he said, 'No, I'm lost.' The sky was overcast and after all the turnings around we had done it was difficult to decide which way to go. After a while we came upon a road, which seemed to be going somewhere, so we took it and kept driving. Before long we heard music coming over a loud speaker and through the trees we could see an army camp. We decided to go in and ask for directions to get back to Batavia.

As we drove in between the barracks we came to some sort of parade ground with a flag pole in the centre of it flying the red and white insurrection movement's flag. While quite a few Pelopors obviously surprised, were looking at us, we, even more surprised than they were, made a top speed U turn around their flag pole and got the hell out of it as fast as we could. Not a shot was fired. We had been very lucky. We could have had our heads stuck on a bamboo pole on a raft floating down the *kali* in the main street the next day. That's what they did to the Dutch Army men that they could get their hands on.

They would chop their heads off, stick them on poles on a bamboo raft and release the raft at the head of the creek to flow unattended down the length of the main street. Willy and I had been frightened out of our wits that afternoon, but now it was a good laughing point with the boys at drinking time. How Eddie and Willy, pissed out of their mind, had decided to take on the Pelopors by themselves single-handed. I didn't hear the end of it until I left. A couple of weeks later, one night in the barrack, one of the boys came in with good news. He had been to the Headquarters that afternoon and had been told that he could get on one of the ships taking back to Holland the Dutch families who during the war had been in Japanese prison camps. However there was a catch to it. He had to be prepared to help on board. 'Doing what?' we all wanted to know. 'Kind of helping with the kids… organising games. Things like that.' The next morning we all fronted up at the Headquarters and to our general disbelief we were all recruited to help with the kids. The ship was due to leave in five days. We had to report on board the night before it left to assist the boarding passengers. The ship was a war-time troop transport fitted with bunks instead of hammocks, like the *Eastern Prince*. Boarding the night before it was due to leave gave us the choice of bunks. We all grouped ourselves together one deck down in a well-ventilated corner in the men's section.

We were told that male and female were to be separated. Men and boys in one place and women, girls and toddlers of either sex in another place. The next day we were to act as ushers and help with the luggage. That night we ate in the galley. Our meal was a feast. It was unbelievable, a real gourmet package. As if it had been prepared by some world famous chef. As we commented on it we were told that the food was going to be like that for the rest of the voyage. These people had been starving in Japanese prison camps since 1942 and now deserved nothing but the best. They had to be rebuilt to look like normal human beings again. And since we were getting the same food it suited us also. We kind of felt rewarded for having had to put up with the army's emergency rations of rice and sardines.

# 23

# BACK TO EUROPE

## 1947

By 6am the poor wretches started to arrive. The boarding was orderly and peaceful enough. And as to the helping with the luggage these poor devils did not have very much and what they did have they did not want to be separated from so most of them carried their own. They had been brought to the wharf by buses and trucks and by early afternoon we were ready to go. Two hours later the ship gently slipped out of Batavia harbour and headed west. When dinnertime came the food was dished out on plates from the galley and all could have as much as they wanted and come back for more as many times as they wished. That night no one seemed to want to go to bed. They were all on deck. We, the army boys, were flirting with some of the older girls, it was sad to hear some of their stories. Most of them said that they had not been maltreated by the Japs, only that there had been no food or very little of it. That was still evident nearly a year after they had been freed. Some of them did not look too bad but many of them still had that cadaverous look of malnutrition. Strangely enough most of them did not eat much. It looked as if their long internment had somehow permanently destroyed their appetite. As well as three delicious healthy meals every day there was always plenty of cakes and chocolates for morning and afternoon teas and for late night supper, but they did not seem to be overly anxious to partake.

The younger kids screamed and ran around all day but the older ones were more subdued. There was an aura of sadness and melancholy about them all. It was quite understandable; after all they were now on their way to the other side of the world to a place called Holland. Most of them knew it as the mother country but had never set foot in it. Most of these families had been in the Dutch East Indies for generations. They were now on their way to a place they didn't really know. To a strange place of which all they knew was the language. They wanted to know all about it. I personally could not help much. I had grown up in Marseilles and had not been to Holland since I was a little baby. Hence the days passed. As it turned out we did not have to make ourselves useful very much. The kids knew what to do and organised their own games and entertainment, while the adults, quite independently, socialised amongst themselves. We, the army boys, used to congregate in the gun turrets. There were two of them, one forward and one aft. The guns of course had been taken off but the turrets were still there. Kids were not allowed to come up there. At night we often used to invite some of the older girls up there for a chat and a drink. Sometimes the entertainment went a lot further than what had been expected. Still we were young and we lived life to the full. Our military war experience had taught us to face any eventuality and never to walk away from any situation. So we were quite prepared to comply with the desires of these lovely young ladies anxious to appease their gnawing amorous starvation imposed by their long confinement in the Japanese prison camps. And so the trip went on. The weather was fine, the food was great and the girls divine. After about three and a half weeks we reached Suez at the southern end of the Suez Canal. There we stopped for a few days and we went ashore. One of the boys had arranged with a taxi to take us to Cairo to have a look at the pyramids. We left early one morning driving most of the way along the Canal. Every time we stopped we were mobbed by dozens of itinerant merchants wanting to sell us their goods. All sorts of things. From bananas to genuine, excavated archaeological treasures. We of course at that age were not interested. All we wanted was to see the pyramids and the Sphinx and we did.

Today, Cairo extends all the way to the pyramids. Buses, on wide bitumen roads, take the tourists right up to the entrance. But in those days the plateau of Giza was way out in the desert, miles from Cairo. We drove a part of the way and then went on by camel. It was a lot of fun but we were disappointed when we got there. We couldn't go inside. Before we left the driver had told us that we could, but obviously that was another con to get a full day hire. Nevertheless we did enjoy the trip. While we had been away to see the pyramids, the passengers had been taken to a warehouse where they had been outfitted with winter

215

clothing. They had been taken there by bus and as we came on board that night we found them all showing each other their various selections. Apparently there was a lot to choose from, and it was all paid for by the Dutch Government. That night the Captain told us that since we were being discharged from the army we should go to that warehouse to be issued with a civilian outfit. And so the next day, with some of the passengers who had missed out the day before, we went to this clothing warehouse. It was a new experience. We were given two sets of winter underwear, a pair of shoes, three shirts, a suit, and an overcoat or a trench coat and a tie. We could choose. I picked a light blue woollen herringbone suit and a cream trench coat. Of course we were still in the army and even though we were dying to don our new outfits we were not as yet allowed to do so. But of course we did.

There was no one on board to scrutinise military discipline. It felt funny to be a civilian again.

And then the voyage resumed. The next morning early we went through the Suez Canal. It took most of the day and that night we were in the Mediterranean heading west again. Two days later at sunset we passed Gibraltar and I realised then that I had been all the way around the world at Queen Wilhemina's expense. It took another three weeks to get to Holland. Early one morning when I went on deck I could see that we already had entered the canal to Amsterdam. We tied up at about 11am. We all had lunch and in the afternoon the disembarkation started. It was quite hectic. Every one was confused. Kids were running all over the place. Their parents had no idea what to do or what was to come next. For an hour or so it was a shambles.

Eventually the ex-internees were assembled in various groups by the local officials and sent to different addresses in Amsterdam where they could settle down and start a new life. Transport had been arranged for them. No one, however, had been instructed to tell us army boys where to go. Apparently they did not even know that we were on board.

These officials were all civilians, welfare officers; they had absolutely nothing to do with the army. And so, after all the ex-internees had been taken care of, and a lot of arguing with the civilian officials had taken place we were finally sent with a couple of taxis to a kind of boarding house called Huis Lydia in down town Amsterdam. By then it was already dark and late at night. We each got a room and arranged to meet the next morning to decide what to do. After breakfast we decided to report to Headquarters to let them know that we had arrived. All the boys were anxious to get home even if, for the time being, only on leave. I did also. The Netherlands East Indies Army Headquarters was in The Hague the capital of the Netherlands, about an hour and a half away by train from Amsterdam. So away we went. Standing room only on the train but it was a short trip and the scenery was beautiful. When we arrived at The Hague it took us a long time to find the Headquarters. When we finally did and fronted at the inquiry counter the attendant who was a civilian had no idea where to send us. He disappeared for nearly an hour and when he came back he did not seem to be any the wiser. He sent us to see a Colonel who was not of the East Indies Army and the poor old fellow although very nice and trying to be helpful had absolutely no idea what to do with us.

We all told him that what we needed first was money and then a leave pass to go home for a while. He easily understood that but apparently he had no authority to comply with our request. After he made a few phone calls we all got some money and a three-week leave pass The money wasn't very much and we were made to sign for it. Apparently no one knew that we were there or that we were coming. All the other boys got a train voucher to go to their respective hometown but I didn't. My home was in Marseilles, in France, another country. The old fellow didn't know what to do about me. He asked me to come back the next day.

When I saw him the following morning he was very nice to me. The day before he had been very officious in front of all of us but this time he asked me to sit down and we had a cup of coffee. He explained to me that in Holland things were not quite settled down properly yet. He said that Holland was now sending troops to the East Indies rather than demobilising them. I told him that I knew that, I said to him that it was the reason why we had to volunteer to make ourselves 'useful' on the ship in order to get back to Holland. He laughed and asked me about my father. He knew he was the Consul in Marseilles and he told me that my father was the one who would eventually give me my final discharge papers. He also gave me a one way train ticket to Paris and another one from Paris to Marseilles. A few days later I rang my father to tell him that I would arrive in Marseilles by train the next day at about lunchtime.

As the train pulled up at Saint Charles railway station in Marseilles I looked out of the window and I could see my father, my mother my brother Phil and my little brother Doudou.

They were standing at the end of the platform, scrutinising the passengers exiting the train. When I came out they saw me and waving their hands they hurried over towards me. My mother hugged and kissed me, then my father shook my hand and for quite a while wouldn't let go of it. My little brother took my army cap off my head and donned it proud as Punch. My mother pointing to the little ribbons on my uniform said, 'Oh, you've been decorated.' All this exuberance went on for quite a while. Eventually my father said, 'Let's go home.' And so we did. It was early 1947, I had just turned twenty. I had been away from home for five years. The first few days were very pleasant. We talked about what had happened in Marseilles while I was away. We talked about Australia and the places where I had been in the Pacific. We talked about the end of the war in Europe and finally we talked about what I intended to do now that the war was over. I had originally applied to be discharged in order to pursue my studies. Even after I had written that letter in Timor I had often wondered if it had really been my intention to do that or had it simply been a reluctance to play toy soldiers in a post war era which had no more real excitement to offer.

I could not see myself going to university to achieve a profession that would sit me behind a desk for the rest of my life. It hurt me just to think about it. I was back home with my family, the same place where I had grown up, with the same people who loved me and with whom I had spent all my life until I went away. Why was it not the same as before? Now the Germans were gone, food was plentiful again, we had all lived through it, we had survived; everything was back to normal. Why was I so depressed? I couldn't explain it. I knew that I had to do something but I did not know what. Anything I contemplated seemed so trivial, so pointless, so unimportant. Was I to spend the rest of my life engaged in some worthless exercise that would achieve nothing? Some dull, pitiful job which offered no excitement and no personal satisfaction? And even when it came to that I had no idea what personal satisfaction I was longing for.

One night after dinner I went to my father's study and we had a long talk. I tried to explain to him how I felt but I couldn't. I just couldn't find the words to describe exactly how I felt. I could not explain to him this kind of emotional vacuum in which I found myself immersed. I could not describe the problems that were gnawing at me, when in fact I should have been happy to be back home safe and sound with my parents and my brothers ready to start my life all over again. The more I tried to explain it to him the more hopeless it sounded to me and probably the more silly it must have sounded to him.

Years later I realised that at the time my father knew more about the way I felt than I did myself. His advice had been, 'Give it time.' I thought him then to be quite indifferent to my plight when in fact his life experience had wisely encompassed all my dilemma and frustration and had come up with the sole appropriate solution. He was right of course but it took me nearly six years of time giving, before I realised that he was right. Before I left Holland I had been told that my discharge papers would eventually be sent to the Consulate in Marseilles and that I would then be discharged by the local Consul. That meant my father. He would be the one who eventually would discharge me but before he could do it he would have to receive the documents giving him the authority to do it. It also meant of course that my father was now militarily in charge of me until my documents arrived. How long was it going to take? Neither he nor I had any idea but I told him that until l was officially discharged I was still in the army and consequently still entitled to my pay.

'So what are you going to do in the mean time?'

'Nothing… just wait.' It immediately dawned on me that my reply did not fit into my father's overall concept. Getting paid for doing nothing was not a notion that my father could easily contemplate. A few days later he saw to it. He contacted the American military H.Q. in Marseilles and asked them if they could use me until my discharge documents arrived. What do you think they said? The next day I was taking inventories of all sorts of junk at an ex-German submarine base at l'Estaque, near Marseilles.

The base was a huge big reinforced concrete building built by the Germans during the war to house and repair submarines. I was being picked up every morning by Jeep and taken there for the day. I had to list miles of cables of different sizes and thousands of spare parts which I had no idea what they were for let alone what to call them. When I asked the American Major who was in charge of the place what I should do about it he replied nonplussed 'Call them anything you want, just invent some names… who cares?' So once again in my military career I had to revert to my 'practical' skills. You'd laugh yourself numb at some of the names I did come up with. In spite of my intimate emotional problems my social life in Marseilles was quite active. My mother was always very anxious to show me off in my uniform to all her friends and particularly their daughters. I was invited to parties all over the place. And frankly I did enjoy myself. One Sunday at one of these parties I was talking to a girl whose boyfriend was also Dutch. She introduced me to him. He came from Rotterdam and we got talking. He told me that he was in Marseilles on his way to North Africa to buy camels. Camels? What on earth did he want camels for? 'For the zoo, the Rotterdam Zoo'. Apparently during the war, because of the scarcity of food, zoo animals had to be destroyed. Now that the war was over all the zoos in Europe were trying to restore their stocks. Hence he was on his way to North Africa.

'Are you a zoologist?' I asked him. No he wasn't. He told me that a friend of his father worked at the zoo and that was how he got this job. At 7am I was back at the Marseilles' Saint Charles railway station boarding a train to Paris on my way to Rotterdam. I was still in the army and through my father's benevolence I was still detailed to the American army to take inventories at the ex-German submarine base at l'Estaque. It took a lot of convincing my father that in all fairness I should be given time off in order to secure some kind of employment now that I was about to be discharged. Naturally he saw this as an attempt to escape from the submarine base, and of course he was right; no, only partially right, but a job catching animals for zoos for the first time appealed to me. In the end he had given in and now I was comfortably seated in a train, travelling north through France hoping to secure an interview for a job which I didn't know if it really existed. I arrived in Rotterdam very early the next day. I had a cup of coffee and breakfast at the railway station and when the time came I went to the zoo. It was called Blijdorp and it would open at 10am. I did not want to be there too early. It would have seemed as if I was anxious, which of course I was. So I waited until thirty seconds past ten and then knocked on the office door. I was let in and told that the director might not be there for another hour or so. It didn't matter, I'd wait.

When he arrived I introduced myself and was invited to his office. I told him about the chap I had met in Marseilles on his way to buy camels in North Africa. I told him that I had served in the Netherlands East Indies Army and had seen action in New Guinea and Borneo and Timor. That I was used to jungle conditions and that catching birds and animals was the sort of job that I knew I could do. He was very nice and friendly but apologetically explained that it wasn't really a job. It was more like a one-off contract to supply the zoo with animals. I would not be a zoo employee. I would be paid a small retainer for the duration of the contract but the real money would come from what I would catch and send to them. He told me that they were anxious to get a lot of animals and birds particularly from South America. If that sort of thing interested me, he said that they would be prepared to offer me a contract for any kind of South American animal or bird I could catch. If that sort of thing interested me? Are you kidding? I was beside myself. Of course I was interested. I could already see myself in jodhpurs and boots ahead of my team slashing our way through the Amazon jungle in the 'bring them back alive' business. Of course I had to get there first. And I would need transport, and men and traps and…and…and…and so many other things. And

223

obviously first of all I would need money. And quite a bit of it. I had with me all my military papers and with them my pay book. It showed that I had not received any money since I had gone to Seymour two years before. My pay even then had been over thirty-two pounds a month. A hell of a lot more than the seven shillings a day that the Australian colonel in Seymour had told the paymaster to give us while we were there with the Australian Army. At the time we had no facilities to bank so we all carried our money with us wherever we went. By then I already had quite a lot of cash on me, and nothing except a few odds and ends from the canteen to spend it on. So I had let it mount up in my pay book.

With all my succeeding promotions I knew that by now the Netherlands East Indies Army was owing me quite a lot of money. So that afternoon I took a train to Den Haag, The Hague. There I went straight to the old colonel that we had seen when we first arrived in Holland. I told him that I wanted all the money that was owing to me. I showed him my pay book and he agreed that obviously I had a lot of money coming to me. He of course had no authority to give me any. It depended, according to him, on the *Ministerie van Buitenlandse Zaken*. The Department of External Affairs of which the KNIL was a part. He asked me to leave my pay book with him and that he would see to it that the matter be settled. That night I was on my way back to Marseilles and the submarine base minus my pay book. But be that as it may, by then I had decided what I was going to do in this dull post-war existence. I was going to be a big game hunter in the 'bring them back alive' business.

I had the money to set myself up. I had the jungle experience to organise what it was going to take, and I had the guts to carry it through. The next morning when I arrived in Marseilles I went straight to the Consulate to see my father. I told him about the zoo and the business I intended to get myself into. At first he laughed his head off then more subdued I could see that he did not really believe me to be so stupid. In fact until the afternoon, a month and a half later, when I boarded the boat leaving Marseilles, I could still see in his demeanour that he thought that the whole thing was some kind of a joke.

Now, of course, time was of the essence. I wanted to be discharged immediately so that I could arrange my new business. It had been decided that I would return to the zoo in a couple of weeks' time to sign the contract and organise the final details. I asked my father to inquire about my discharge so that I could plan ahead. He did not seem to have much success. The Dutch Department of Foreign Affairs did not appear to be very anxious to get rid of me. They kept procrastinating with a lot of letters which seemed to be missing the point altogether. At that stage I even got the impression that they had changed their mind and had decided to keep me in the army and send me back to Java. After all, the liberation movement in Java was becoming more and more active and Holland was sending more and more Dutch forces to the Dutch East Indies to relieve the tension. Since I was still in the KNIL it sounded likely that I could be included in one of these transports. That is what my father thought and I must agree, at the time, it made sense. After two weeks of taking inventories again at the submarine base I returned to Rotterdam and fronted up at the zoo as it had been arranged. I had to explain the uncertainty of my military situation. We talked about it. The Director of the zoo and his assistant were quite confident that my discharge would come through. Later that morning I was shown all over the zoo. Then back at the office I was shown pictures of birds and animals that had been guests of the zoo before the war and that now they were hoping to re-acquire. We came across some photographs of kangaroos and I told them that I saw plenty of them in Australia when we were driving between Brisbane and Casino. They were stupefied. They had no idea that I had been to Australia during the war. They, of course, were very anxious to get a lot of Australian animals and birds.

They therefore assumed that since I had been in Australia during the war I knew all there was to know about Australian birds and animals. Their reaction was, 'Forget South America go to Australia instead… you know the place, it will make it very easy for you'. At first I wasn't at all convinced. South America sounded more exciting. I had never been there. I had read books about it and about the Amazon jungle. About Colonel Fawcett and his entire expedition who had disappeared in it never to be seen or heard of again. It sounded fascinating but all that knowledge was only from books. Besides I did not speak Portuguese or Spanish whereas in Australia they spoke English. It had its merits. It was a bit of a dilemma but in the end, since this was going to be the first of what I hoped would be many assignments, I took their advice and opted for Australia. South America would come later. The next morning I took a train to The Hague. I wanted my money. There I went to see the old colonel with whom I had left my pay book. He told me that he had sent it to the Department of Foreign Affairs and that if I went there I would get my money. I was told where to go and there I went. After being tossed around from one office to another for the rest of the morning, I finally landed in front of a sergeant major who had received my pay book and knew about my wanting to be paid the outstanding balance. He told me to sit down and went to get my back pay. When he came back the amount he had with him was no way near the amount that I had worked out was owing to me. Of course I blew up and the poor devil wanted to know why. I took my book and showed him when last I had received any money. And that had been in Seymour, Australia when the Australian colonel had us paid at the Australian Army rate. That amount had been entered in the book and that had been the last entry in it.

The sergeant major left me again in his office and went to seek further advice. When he came back he explained apologetically that, according to their records, all I was due was my pay from the 23 July 1945 to the present day. That was when Eitsick and I came back to Brisbane from Seymour. He said that before that date I had been attached to the Australian Army and that therefore I must have been paid by the Australian paymaster. I told him that that was ridiculous. I again pointed at the last entry in my pay book. That had been at the Junior Leader School way back in February 1945. I told him that I had not asked for any pay since because I didn't need any. I told him that now I wanted to be paid for all the time I had been in Seymour and New Guinea and Morotai and Tarakan and Canungra, right up to now and then later right to the day of my disharge. He was very sorry but he said that the records showed that I and the other boys had been transferred to the Australian

Army and that the KNIL had no records of us for that period of time. Of course that wasn't right and I told him with all the appropriate expletives necessary to enrich my outburst. He was quite adamant that the records were correct and that I could, if I wished, take the matter further independently with the Australian government. He assured me that there was no mistake and kindly suggested that in the mean time I should take what money he had for me and leave it at that. I, frothing at the mouth, told him to 'shove' his money and stormed out of his office without taking a single cent. Back in Marseilles I told my father all about it. He offered to take the matter further officially through the Consulate. I explained to him that if we did not front up to the paymaster on pay days, what was coming to us would stay suspended and could be claimed later. I told him that in the islands we didn't need any money or very little, so we didn't claim any. I explained that we were very well looked after and that there was nothing for us to spend money on.

True to his offer he wrote an official letter to the appropriate authorities in Holland. When a reply came, it was in line with what the sergeant major had told me in Holland. That we boys had been transferred to the Australian Army to be trained as officers. That for that period of time we did depend entirely from it. That we had probably been issued with an Australian pay book and that for that period of time the Dutch East Indies Army had absolutely no record of us. They claimed it was evidenced by the pay I had received from the Australian paymaster when I first went to Seymour. That was the reduced pay that the Australian colonel had imposed.

I knew and admitted to my father that I had received that one amount but I also showed him that that entry had been the last. There were none after that. And we had not been issued with any Australian pay book

After a lot of discussion I finally convinced my father to take the matter up again. My argument was that since that first entry of the reduced pay by the Australian Army was stamped in my KNIL pay book it proved that we had not been issued with an Australian pay book. And that since no further entries were stamped in it after that, it did prove that I had not received any more money from the Australian Army. If I had, the amounts would also have been entered in the same pay book but there were no other entries there. My father saw the logic of my argument and dispatched further correspondence to that effect. By now the situation had become somewhat embarrassing. I was running out of money. Perhaps I should have taken the money that the sergeant major had suggested instead of blowing my top and walking out. Meanwhile I was still assiduously making inventory at the German submarine base and could therefore have demanded to be paid for it. Either by my father or whoever else it was in the American Army who had to come up with it. However I did not want to do that; I wanted all my back pay to come in one single lot. My claim was more solid that way.

I knew that I wasn't the only one in such a predicament. My friend Eitsick had done the same thing. At the schools and in the islands we had no need for money. For the little we needed we had enough cash in our pockets. Then when we left Australia on our way to Timor the war ended. It was time to start thinking. We both decided that it would be wise to start saving for civilian life again. So we did not ask for money. We just let it mount up. But now I wanted it and I was not going to let them get away with it with the excuse that they had no record of me while I had been transferred to the Australian army to do my officer's training. After all they could still check with the commanding officers at Camp Columbia, at Hollandia and at Morotai.

Back in Marseilles I had made preparations to organise my voyage to Australia for my first contract with the zoo. I had booked a passage with the Messagerie Maritime in Marseilles on a ship called the *Ville d'Amiens*. It was due to sail in October for the French Carribean Islands then Panama, Tahiti, Noumea and finally Sydney. I had acquainted myself with all the different Australian animals and birds that I could find in photographs. My mother had prepared for me an elaborate first aid kit, which weighed almost as much as all the rest of my luggage. I had made a good attempt at reading as much about Australia as I could find in the public library in Marseilles. The zoo had given me a whole pile of official introductory letters and documents to facilitate things and circumvent red tape on my arrival in Australia.

My father on his side had been in active contact with the Department of External Affairs in Holland trying to expedite my discharge and secure what was owing to me. I was all set to go except for these two things. Only a couple of days before the *Ville d'Amiens* was due to leave Marseilles my father struck oil. I was at home. He rang me in the middle of the morning to tell me that my discharge had come through, which was nice, and that my pay, the whole lot of it, had been sent to the Barclay Bank's branch in Marseilles, which was even nicer. He told me that I could go and pick it up anytime I wanted to. So I was there before lunch. It was all there all right, except for the money that the Dutch colonel had given us when we first arrived in Holland and we were given three weeks leave. That amount had been deducted. There was no explanation as to why all of a sudden they had finally discovered that all that money was indeed due to me. I have many times suspected that the matter was settled in reference to my father's persistence rather than through intimate official channels or freshly discovered records.

On the due date, in mid-afternoon of that October day of 1947, leaning over the railings, I found myself frantically waving goodbye to my parents and my brothers standing on the quay.

Six weeks later, after an unbelievable voyage, I landed in Sydney. I was back in Australia This time ready to catch all different kinds of animals and birds for the zoos of Europe.

# 24

# AT HOME IN
# AUSTRALIA

## 1947–

For about three and a half years I did just that and made a
lot of money at it. I went to northern New South Wales
and caught kangaroos and wombats at Mount Duval north of
Armidale. Then I went into the Pilliga Scrub west of Gunnedah
where I caught a lot of emus, kangaroos, wallabies, possums,
goannas, snakes, black and sulphur-crested cockatoos and galahs.
After that I went to Queensland: Brisbane, Roma, the Carnavon
Range, Springsure, Emerald and the Nogoa River. There I
caught red kangaroos, more emus, a lot of birds, carpet, black
and brown snakes, more goannas, frilled and blue tongue lizards
and even a few echidnas. I never took any koalas, they could not
be fed in Europe. I also sent a lot of mountain lorikeets,

magpies, kookaburras, quarians and different breeds of finches to the zoo.

I never did go to South America. I stayed in Australia instead. I fell in love with the place and its people. I made Australia my home. I became an Australian citizen. I was no longer a foreigner. I got married and fathered three sons. And by the way, I did eventually resume my studies. I went to the University of Queensland and secured a Bachelor of Arts degree. Later I studied law and was admitted as a barrister of the Supreme Court of Queensland, New South Wales and the High Court of Australia.

Today I am the old grandfather of eleven grandchildren and five step-grandchildren. I am a retired fair dinkum Aussie still enjoying a nice fruitful life full of excitement and surprises, a nice cold beer when it's hot, and a large whisky every night before dinner. And it's all I want.

# GLOSSARY

**ATS**  Auxiliary Territorial Services. Women's auxiliary in the army.

**Boche**  Derogatory name given by the French to the German soldiers, starting in 1914.

*Confrère*  Fellow members of the same profession.

**Duck**  A floating vehicle with a propeller and four wheels. They were used for landing material. Some were as large as a truck others were the size of a Jeep.

**GMC**  General Motor Corporation trucks used by the army.

*gnole*  homemade brandy.

*kali*  A creek

*kampong*  A village

*kapala kampong*  The head of a village.

*kerbou*  Buffalo

**KNIL**  Koninklijk Nederlandsch Indisch Leger (Royal Netherlands Indies Army).

**LSI**  Landing Ship Infantry.

**LST**  Landing Ship Tank.

*Maquis*  The fighting French force inside France during the German Occupation.

**Pelopors**  The name given to the Indonesian Freedom Fighters.

**POW**  Prisoner of War.

**RAF**  Royal Air Force.

*sate*  Pieces of meat skewed on thin bamboo sticks.

*sopy*  Alcohol made from distilled coconut milk.

**Sten Gun** A small hand-held gun that could fire single shots or rapid fire at will. It had a magazine that held 28 nine milimetre bullets.

**USO** United Service Organization. To provide morale, welfare and recreation type services to uniformed military personnel

**WAAF** Women's Auxiliary Air Force. Women auxiliary in the RAF.

# INDEX

237